John Gordon Swift MacNeill

How the Union was Carried

John Gordon Swift MacNeill

How the Union was Carried

ISBN/EAN: 9783337061326

Printed in Europe, USA, Canada, Australia, Japan

Cover: Foto ©ninafisch / pixelio.de

More available books at **www.hansebooks.com**

HOW THE UNION

WAS CARRIED

BY

J. G. SWIFT MACNEILL, M.A., M.P.,

CHRIST CHURCH, OXFORD; BARRISTER AT LAW; PROFESSOR OF CONSTITUTIONAL AND
CRIMINAL LAW IN THE HONOURABLE SOCIETY OF THE KING'S INNS, DUBLIN;
AUTHOR OF "THE IRISH PARLIAMENT, WHAT IT WAS, AND WHAT
IT DID," AND OF "ENGLISH INTERFERENCE
WITH IRISH INDUSTRIES."

LONDON:
KEGAN PAUL, TRENCH & CO., 1 PATERNOSTER SQUARE.
1887.

CONTENTS.

	PAGE
INTRODUCTION	1

CHAPTER I.
THE MOTIVE FOR THE UNION . . . 7

CHAPTER II.
THE ADMINISTRATION AND RECALL OF LORD FITZ-WILLIAM 20

CHAPTER III.
A SYSTEM OF HORRORS 30

CHAPTER IV.
THE REBELLION OF 1798 AND THE ENGLISH GOVERNMENT 42

CHAPTER V.
MILITARY FORCE AND THE UNION . . 50

CHAPTER VI.
ROBBERY, TORTURE, MURDER, AND THE UNION 58

CHAPTER VII.
THE UNION AND EXCEPTIONAL LEGISLATION AND MARTIAL LAW 71

CHAPTER VIII.
THE CIRCUMSTANCES ATTENDING THE FIRST INTRODUCTION OF THE UNION TO THE IRISH PARLIAMENT . 78

CHAPTER IX.
THE DEFEAT OF THE UNION IN 1799 . . . 88

CHAPTER X.
SOME OF THE MEANS BY WHICH THE UNION WAS CARRIED 93

CHAPTER XI.
THE COMPETENCY OF THE IRISH PARLIAMENT TO PASS THE UNION 153

INTRODUCTION.

IRELAND was deprived of her native Parliament by means which intensify the desire of the Irish people for the restoration of their legislative independence. A recurrence to what has been termed ancient history is deprecated in certain quarters; but as the Bishop of Chester has well said, "the roots of the present lie deep in the past."[1] "There is," says Mr Butt, "a sense in which it matters very little how we lost our Parliament, but there is another in which it matters a great deal. The Irishman believes, and truly believes, that its Parliament was wrested from his country by fraud and violence unparalleled in the history of the world. The feelings of nations are facts with which statesmen who know anything of statesmanship must deal. The sense of national pride, the traditions which nations cherish in their inmost souls, the memories of bygone wrongs, the recollections of former greatness and former good—all these are realities which it were a miserable statesmanship to neglect. They make up the soul and spirit of the nation with which you have to deal. You must take them into account just as much as you would the physical condition or capabilities of a country." "It is impossible to separate a nation from that past history which is a part of its existence. The attempt is as vain as it would be in the case of an individual. The man is made up of the memories of his

[1] Stubbs' "Constitutional History of England," i., preface.

life, of the character they form, and the passions and principles to which they give life; and the Ireland of to-day, the Ireland which British statesmen have to conciliate, is an Ireland upon which are impressed the memories of her prosperous and glorious independence, and of the terrible and cruel wrongs by which that independence was destroyed."[1] Mr Fox, in 1806, characterised the Union as "atrocious in its principle and abominable in its means." "It was," he said, "a measure the most disgraceful to the Government of the country that was ever carried or proposed."[2] Mr Gladstone is of a similar opinion. "I know," he says, "no blacker or fouler transaction in the history of man, than the making of the Union between England and Ireland."[3] The view of the historian coincides in this matter with the view of the statesman. "There are," says Mr Lecky, "indeed, few things more discreditable to English political literature than the tone of palliation or even of eulogy that is usually adopted towards the authors of this transaction. Scarcely any element or aggravation of political immorality was wanting; and the term honour, if it be applied to such men as Castlereagh or Pitt, ceases to have any real meaning in politics. Whatever may be thought of the abstract merits of the arrangement, the Union as it was carried was a crime of the deepest turpitude,—a crime which, by imposing with every circumstance of infamy a new form of government on a reluctant and

[1] "Proceedings of the Home Rule Conference, 1873," pp. 18, 19. I heard Mr Butt speak these words. They were received with enthusiasm by the whole audience, who rose to their feet and cheered for some moments. The Home Rule Conference of 1873 led to the formation of the Irish Parliamentary party.

[2] *Morning Chronicle*, February 4, 1806.

[3] Speech at Liverpool, June 28, 1886.

protesting nation, has vitiated the whole course of Irish opinion."[1]

The opponents of the Union in the Irish Parliament were consoled by the reflection, that sooner or later the verdict of posterity would stigmatise that stupendous crime. "Depend upon it," said Mr Bushe in the Irish House of Commons, "a day of reckoning will come, history will overhaul this transaction."[2] A close investigation of the details of the Union is now impossible. The authors of that measure have purposely destroyed the evidence which would have revealed in clear light the full measure of its iniquity. Mr Ross, the editor of the "Cornwallis Correspondence," while acknowledging his obligations to the persons who had placed materials for the work at his disposal, makes the following observations:—"Many other collections have been as cordially submitted to my inspection, but upon investigation it appeared that such documents as might have thrown additional light on the history of those times, and especially of the Union, had been purposely destroyed. For instance, after a search instituted at Welbeck by the kindness of the Duke of Portland, it was ascertained that the late Duke had burnt all his father's political papers from 1780 to his death. In like manner the Chancellor Lord Clare, Mr Wickham, Mr King, Sir Herbert Taylor, Sir Edward Littlehales, Mr Marsden, the Knight of Kerry, and indeed almost all the persons officially concerned in carrying the Union, appear to have destroyed the whole of their papers. Mr Marsden, by whom many of the arrangements were concluded, left a MS. book containing invaluable details, which was burnt only a

---

[1] "Leaders of Public Opinion in Ireland," p. 182.
[2] January 22nd, 1799.

few years ago by its then possessor. The destruction of so many valuable documents respecting important transactions, cannot but be regarded as a serious loss to the political history of those times."[1] We discover, too, from a note by Mr Ross, accounting for the non-appearance of a document, that it "must have been destroyed with the great mass of Lord Cornwallis's papers relating to the Union, as it cannot be found."[2]

It is a rule of law and a rule of common-sense, that all things are to be presumed against the destroyer of evidence. His conduct is attributed to the supposed knowledge that the truth would have operated against him.[3] Mr Dundas (Lord Melville), an intimate friend of Mr Pitt's, a member of his Cabinet, and one of the "statesmen of the Union," was in 1805 impeached for malversation of public money. It was found on investigation that his accounts and vouchers had been destroyed. A few sentences of Sir Samuel Romilly's argument in his case will, in this connection, warrant quotation. "I ask your Lordships whether, if any doubt upon the prosecutor's evidence remains upon your minds, it is possible that your Lordships should not, from the destruction of these vouchers, presume the defendant guilty of everything we impute to him? I should think it would be hardly necessary to your Lordships collectively, I am sure it cannot to many of you individually, to state what inferences courts of justice always draw from the destruction of evidence." "In civil cases, a party who destroys evidence of a transaction is always charged to the full extent that it was possible that that transaction could have gone." "I am sure that no case occurs of any person convicted of an

---

[1] "Cornwallis Correspondence," i., preface p. vi.   [2] *Ibid.*, iii. p. 197.
[3] "Taylor on Evidence," 8th ed., i. 137, 138.

offence upon circumstantial evidence in which the court does not act upon presumptions exactly of the same kind." "I submit that a man standing in the situation in which Lord Melville stands—a public accountant, a trustee for the public, a man who had used part of the public money, as he himself states, not for the purposes for which it had been placed in his hands, but for other purposes—I say it was peculiarly his duty to preserve his accounts, and that the destruction of his accounts and vouchers is of itself a crime which would alone be a just subject of impeachment."[1]

In these pages I will endeavour to sketch in outline the general features of the method by which the Union was carried. The picture, for the reasons I have stated, can never be fully filled up. In describing the motive of the English Government in proposing the Union, and the means by which that measure was effected, I will, as far as possible, quote the observations of public men in the British and the Irish Parliaments on matters

---

[1] Cobbett's "State Trials," xxix. 1193-1196. The ballad literature of the period ascribes to Mr Dundas a prominent place in the transactions of the Union. The chorus of one of the anti-Union songs runs thus—

"Give Pitt and Dundas and Jenkins a glass,
Who'd ride on John Bull and make Paddy an ass."

"Who," says the Rev. Professor Galbraith, S.F.T.C.D., "was the man that helped, in the most laborious, and, I am sorry to say, efficacious way, his friend William Pitt to carry the resolutions through the English House of Commons, the object of which was to rob us of our nationality? Dundas, the First Lord of the Admiralty. In 1804, three years after this, when he occupied the post of First Lord of the Admiralty, under the title of Lord Melville, his name was struck off the Privy Council, much to the regret of his friend Pitt, who could not, however, help him. Why? Because he robbed the public money. Mr Whitbred had him impeached, and his bosom friend, Mr Pitt, was obliged to advise His Majesty to expel him from the Privy Council."—"Proceedings of the Home Rule Conference," 1873, p. 75.

which came prominently before them. I will also rely on some extracts from the correspondence of Lords Cornwallis and Castlereagh, which, though carefully expurgated, contain startling admissions of the charges brought against these noblemen by the opponents of the Union in both countries.

HOW THE UNION WAS CARRIED.

CHAPTER I.

THE MOTIVE FOR THE UNION.

"I OPENLY assert," said Mr O'Connell, when speaking in his own defence in the Court of Queen's Bench in Ireland during the State Trials of 1844—"I openly assert that I cannot endure the Union, because it is founded upon the greatest injustice and based on the grossest insult: from an intolerance of Irish prosperity. These were the motives that induced the malefactors who perpetrated that iniquity; and I have the highest authority—an ornament for years of that Bench—now, although recently, in his honoured grave—for saying that the motive for carrying the Union was an intolerance of Irish prosperity."[1] The personage to

[1] *R. v. O'Connell*, p. 601. The charge was one "of conspiracy," says Mr Lecky, "or in other words of the employment of seditious language against O'Connell, his son, and five of his principal followers." "A great number of charges have been brought against this trial, which have elicited much controversy. It is sufficient to state the facts that are admitted. An error, which at least one Irish judge believed not to have been unintentional, was made in the panel of the jury, and by this error more than twenty Catholics were excluded from the juror list. Of the Catholics whose names were called all were objected to by the government prosecutor, and accordingly there was not a single Roman Catholic on the jury which tried the greatest Catholic of his age in the metropolis of an essentially

whom Mr O'Connell thus alluded was Mr Bushe, who was for eighteen years Solicitor-General under a Tory Administration, and for twenty years Chief-Justice of Ireland. Mr Bushe, speaking in the Irish House of Commons on the 16th January 1800, during one of the debates on the Union, used this language: "You are giving up your independence. To whom? To a nation which for six hundred years has treated you with uniform oppression and injustice. The Treasury Bench startles at the assertion—*non meus hic sermo est*. If the Treasury Bench scold *me*, Mr Pitt will scold *them;* it is his assertion in so many words in his speech. Ireland, says he, has always been treated with injustice and illiberality.[1] Ireland, says Junius, has been uniformly plundered and oppressed. This is not the slander of Junius or the candour of Pitt—it is history. For centuries have the British Parliament and nation kept you down, shackled your commerce and paralysed your exertions; despised your characters and ridiculed your pretensions to any privileges, commercial or

Catholic country, and at a time when sectarian animosity was at its height. After a charge from the Chief Justice, which Macaulay afterwards compared to the displays of judicial partisanship in the State trials of Charles II., O'Connell was found guilty, and condemned to two years' imprisonment, together with a fine, a sentence against which he appealed to the Lords." "The appeal to the House of Lords was heard in September 1844." "The five Law Lords who were present first delivered their opinions, two of them confirming the sentence of the Irish Court, three of them condemning it. Lord Denman in the course of his judgment stigmatised the proceedings in Ireland in the strongest language."—Lecky's "Leaders of Public Opinion," pp. 313-315. Lord Denman said: "If such practices as have taken place in the present instance in Ireland shall continue, the trial by jury will become a mockery, a delusion, and a snare."

[1] Mr Bushe is probably referring to Mr Pitt's speech in the British House of Commons on the Commercial Propositions in 1785. "Parliamentary Register," xvii. p. 249. See also "English Interference with Irish Industries," by J. G. Swift MacNeill.

constitutional. She has never conceded a point to you which she could avoid, or granted a favour which was not reluctantly distilled. They have been all wrung from her like drops of her heart's blood, and you are not in possession of a single blessing, except those which you derive from God, that has not been either purchased or extorted by the virtue of your own Parliament from the illiberality of England."[1] "Throughout the whole career of his long and eventful life, Mr Bushe," says Mr O'Connell, " never retracted one syllable of what he uttered on this subject."[2] Mr Bushe's language is, however, not stronger than that of Mr Grey, who afterwards, as Lord Grey, became Prime Minister of England. His speech in the English House of Commons, on the 21st April 1800, was an echo of Mr Bushe's speech in the Irish House. "Previous to that period (1782)," he says, "they (the Irish) were the most injured and oppressed set of men on the face of the earth."[3]

Previously to 1782 Ireland was injured and oppressed by what Mr Lecky has termed " that great system of commercial restriction which began under Charles II., which under William III. acquired a crushing severity, and which had received several additional clauses in the succeeding reigns."[4] For upwards of two hundred years the English Parliament had enacted a series of laws for the avowed purpose of destroying Irish trade, paralysing Irish industry, and depriving the Irish people of the means of subsistence. The nature and effects of this legislation were thus characterised in the Irish House

[1] "Life of Plunket," by Right Hon. D. Plunket, M.P., ii. p. 354.
[2] "Report of the Discussion in Dublin Corporation on Repeal of the Union, in 1843," p. 34.
[3] Woodfall's "Parliamentary Reports," ii. p. 402.
[4] "England in the Eighteenth Century," iv. p. 501.

of Commons, in October 1779, by Mr Hussey Burgh, who filled the elevated position of Prime Serjeant, and afterwards that of Lord Chief Baron:—"The usurped authority of a foreign Parliament has kept up the most wicked laws that a jealous monopolising ungrateful spirit could desire to restrain the bounty of providence and enslave a nation whose inhabitants are recorded to be a brave, loyal, generous people; by the English code of laws, to answer the most sordid views, they have been treated with a savage cruelty,—the words penalty, punishment, and Ireland are synonymous, they are marked in blood on the margin of their statutes, and though time may have softened the calamities of the nation, the baneful and distinctive influence of these laws have borne her down to a state of Egyptian bondage. The English have sowed their laws like serpents' teeth; they have sprung up as armed men."[1]

Again, previously to 1782 the legislation of the Irish Parliament was controlled by the English and the Irish Privy Councils through the provisions of the celebrated statute known as Poynings' Law. In 1782 that statute was modified, and the Irish Parliament became theoretically independent, but practically as dependent as before on the English Cabinet, who sought to regain by increased corruption the loss of their statutory powers of overriding Irish legislation.[2] The dealings of the English Cabinet with the Irish Parliament were thus, in my opinion, accurately described by Mr Sheridan in the British House of Commons on February 7, 1799, in

[1] MacNevin's "Volunteers," p. 117. For an exposition of the commercial restraints placed on Ireland by the English Parliament, see "English Interference with Irish Industries," by J. G. Swift MacNeill.

[2] For an exposition of the Constitution and Powers of the Irish Parliament see "The Irish Parliament, what it was and what it did," by J. G. Swift MacNeill.

a speech opposing the Union—" I deny what has been so positively asserted, that we have no alternative but division and separation or Union. The real alternative is that the Irish Government should no longer continue to be a corrupt English job. Is it meant to be asserted that there is some innate depravity in the Irish character which makes them unfit to have a Parliament of their own? No, the cause of the corruption which has been complained of is obvious. The government of Ireland has been made a job of for the advantage of English Ministers—this is the corruption, this is the evil which has pervaded it from first to last; but before Ireland be required to surrender her independence, let at least a trial be made of what can be done by an honest Irish Parliament, uninfluenced by a British Minister, by a Parliament having the interest and happiness of Ireland for its object, and looking to Irish prosperity and Irish gratitude for its reward. Let it not be a Parliament looking at St James's only, but one that shall have the advantage of the country constantly in view. Let this experiment at least be tried before the annihilation of the Irish Parliament be proposed. I am certain that nothing can be done in this way which would not strengthen the bonds that unite the two countries."[1]

With all these disadvantages the increase of prosperity in Ireland during the period of her Parliamentary independence (1782-1800) is incontestable, and has been admitted by the foremost advocates of the Union. Lord Clare, the Lord Chancellor of Ireland, to whom, after Mr Pitt and Lord Castlereagh, Ireland is chiefly indebted for the Union, thus writes of this period in 1798—" No nation on the habitable globe advanced in

[1] "Parliamentary Debates," vii. p. 685.

cultivation, in commerce, in agriculture, in manufactures so rapidly in the same period."[1]

The correspondence of Lord Castlereagh goes far, I think, to prove the correctness of Mr Bushe's assertion, that the motive which urged the English Government to pass the Union was an intolerance of Irish prosperity. Mr Knox, assistant private secretary to Lord Castlereagh, and one of his principal agents in the bribery of the Irish Parliament, thus writes to his noble master:— "The worst of it is that some of the strongest points (in favour of the Union) cannot be brought before the public. I have felt this peculiarly this day or two while endeavouring to write upon the subject, and I feel it infinitely easier to say what is true than merely to say what ought to be sent abroad into the world. Farewell, my good lord."[2] The notes of Mr Edward Cooke, "in favour of the Union," have been preserved amongst Lord Castlereagh's papers. This gentleman was Assistant Secretary during the period in which Lord Castlereagh was Chief Secretary to the Lord-Lieutenant, and was likewise actively employed in the direct bribery of Members of Parliament. Mr Cooke's "Notes" supply us with one at least of the points in favour of the Union which could not be brought before the public. "Will the Union," he asks, "make Ireland quiet? Who can judge for the future? Yet although we cannot command futurity, we are to act as if futurity were in our power. We must argue from moral causes to moral effects. If then we are in a disadvantageous situation, we must of course look to the causes which have brought

---

[1] I have collected the principal evidence respecting the prosperity of Ireland during this period in "English Interference with Irish Industries," pp. 97-103.

[2] "Castlereagh Correspondence," ii. p. 45.

us into that situation. What are they?" He then enumerates six causes, placing second on the list, "The general prosperity of the country which has produced great activity and energy."[1] Commenting on this passage in the year 1849, when it was for the first time revealed to the public, Lord Cloncurry thus writes:—
"When the contrivers of the Legislative Union in 1799 avowed to each other in their most secret communications the great object of their work to be a stoppage of the growing prosperity of Ireland, they probably did not dream of so complete an attainment of that end as their successors have achieved in 1849. Their highvaulting ambition has o'erleaped its selle."[2]

An intolerance of Irish prosperity was not, however, the only motive which stimulated the passing of the Union. In 1800 the Irish National Debt was only twenty-one millions, whereas the English National Debt was four hundred and forty-six millions. "If any body," said Mr Curran, "desires to know what would be the consequence of a Union with Great Britain, I will tell him. It would be the emigration of every man of consequence from Ireland; it would be the participation of British taxes without British trade." Mr Johns, speaking in the British House of Commons on the 21st April 1800, feared the cause of the Union was revenue.[3] Half a century previously, a union had been advocated on the ground that, by its means, Ireland would be subject to British taxes. Thus Sir M. Decker writes in 1751:—"By a union with Ireland the taxes on Britain will be lessened for the present, whereby they will contribute to make our goods still cheaper,

---

[1] "Castlereagh Correspondence," iii. pp. 54-55.
[2] "Personal Recollections of Valentine Lord Cloncurry," pp. 471-472.
[3] Woodfall's "Parliamentary Reports," ii. p. 382.

and consequently more vendible. The Irish now pay no taxes to the general, but only to their private support."[1] Again, Mr Postlethwayt writes in 1767, "By the Union, Ireland would soon be enabled to pay a million a year towards the taxes of Great Britain, besides the full support of their own establishment. And would not this in time of war greatly contribute to raise the supplies within the year? And in times of peace might not this, with an addition of a million more on the part of Great Britain, be appropriated as an inviolable debt-paying fund for the redemption of every public incumbrance? By the Union, Ireland would be enabled to assist England with 12,000, if not 15,000 seamen in times of need, which would be a matter of no little importance." Then there comes a passage which displays, I think, a remarkable prescience: "As England does already possess no inconsiderable share of the lands of Ireland, so the Union would prove an effectual method to vest the rest in her; for as the riches of Ireland would chiefly return to England, she continuing the seat of the empire, the Irish landlords would be little better than tenants to her for allowing them the privilege of making the best of their estates."[2]

Dr Johnson once said to an Irish gentleman, "Do not unite with us; we would unite with you only to rob you."[3] Lord Byron opposed the measure in the English House of Lords, characterising it as the "union of the shark with its prey."[4] Mr Cooke, writing to Lord Castlereagh, mentions among the arguments against

---

[1] "Essays on Trade," p. 156.
[2] "Britain's Commercial Interest," pp. 203, 204. I have taken these passages from Mr Battersby's "Repealer's Manual." Dublin, 1833.
[3] Lecky's "Leaders of Public Opinion in Ireland," p. 157.
[4] *Ibid.*, p. 175.

the Union, "We shall be liable to British debts," etc.[1] Lord Castlereagh, writing to the Duke of Portland on the 7th January 1799, assures him that "the proportionate arrangement of the expenses had completely overset the argument on which the enemies of the measure had hitherto principally relied, namely the extension of English debt and taxation to Ireland."[2] Mr Pitt, on 31st January 1799, having no doubt heard the contents of Lord Castlereagh's letter of the 7th, adopted a high moral tone in the English House of Commons. "Sir," he said, "I hope the zeal, the spirit, and the liberal and enlarged policy of this country, has given ample proof that it is not from a pecuniary motive we seek a Union."[3] Mr Sheridan was not, however, reassured. The Irish Members of Parliament, "might perhaps," he said, "have the farther advantage of being transplanted into the Imperial Parliament, of coming into an equal participation of the share of four hundred millions of debt owing by this country."[4] On the 21st of April 1800, Mr Pitt repudiated the notion that the proportionate arrangement, to use Lord Castlereagh's term, would not be religiously observed. "But it had been said, what security can you give to Ireland for the performance of the conditions? If I were asked what security were necessary, without hesitation I would answer, none. The liberality, the justice, the honour of the people of Great Britain have never yet been found deficient."[5] Mr Grey, however, did not take so elevated a view of the situation. "Ireland," he said in the same debate, "can have no security that she shall not be oppressed, unless she pays the very

---

[1] "Castlereagh Correspondence," ii. p. 43.   [2] *Ibid.*, ii. p. 84.
[3] "Parliamentary Debates," vii. p. 656.   [4] *Ibid.*, vii. p. 733.
[5] Woodfall's "Parliamentary Debates," ii. p. 393.

same taxes with Britain. I am far from supposing that the British Members will wantonly abuse their powers, and knowingly make her pay beyond her proportion, but the property of a nation should not be left at the discretion of any man or any set of men who are strangers, however just or generous he or they may be; and it is impossible for Ireland to enjoy that security her constitution at present affords her, if she is united to England in the manner proposed. It is impossible that men should so coolly and dispassionately consider a tax which does not affect themselves, as if they were immediately to pay it; not more than one-sixth of the United Parliament will be Irishmen. We naturally take a pleasure, when in calamitous circumstances, in bringing others into a situation equally deplorable; it is therefore to be apprehended that we would not unwillingly be instrumental in making the burthens of Ireland as heavy as our own."[1] Dr Lawrence, however, accurately foretold the result of the proportionate arrangement. Speaking on 2nd May 1800 in the English House of Commons, he said, "We (England) were to pay off our debts while she (Ireland) would continue to run in debt, until, as in the case of one man going up hill and another going down, we should at last come to what was called a level, and the contributions were to be equalised."[2]

Mr O'Connell in 1843 thus describes the effects of the proportionate arrangement. "At the time of the Union Ireland owed twenty-one millions, England four hundred and forty-six millions. What were the terms of the Union? They were these—that England was to bear for ever the burden of these four hundred and forty-six millions, and consequently for its interest,

---

[1] Woodfall's "Parliamentary Debates," ii. p. 400.
[2] *Ibid.*, ii. p. 592.

and charge the burden of a separate taxation of seventeen millions annually, and that Ireland was not to be charged with the four hundred and forty-six millions at all for its principal and interest.[1] But were these conditions complied with? No, of course they were not; and Ireland now owes every penny of that stupendous sum. You are charged with every fraction of it; and notwithstanding all the distinct promises of Castlereagh, your lands, your properties, your labours, your industry, all, all are liable to be mortgaged for the debt. The notable mode proposed for the equalisation of the debts of the two countries was this—England was to go on paying off her debt until it reached the level of the Irish sum, and this consummation so devoutly to be wished was to be achieved through the instrumentality of the Sinking Fund. But this is only a portion of the juggle, for it is clear that all they wanted was to squeeze as much as they could out of us. I will give you some more of their squeezing. If the Union had been a just and equitable compact, the respective debts should have continued in the same proportion. This, however, was an arrangement too manifestly upright and honest to find countenance with them for a moment, and accordingly Ireland was afflicted by such an indecent spoliation as exposed her to the ridicule of the world. If, when I was a practising barrister, a deed of partnership were brought to me for legal perusal, and that on looking over it I found that the party who was assenting to the deed was a man owing £21,000, who purposed going

---

[1] This was Lord Castlereagh's distinct undertaking. Speaking in the Irish House of Commons on February 5, 1800, he said: "In respect to past expenses Ireland is to have no concern whatever with the debt of Great Britain."

into partnership with a man owing £446,000, and that he was to undertake the liabilities of that partner by virtue of the deed, would I not be inclined to inquire of the attorney in a confidential tone, 'Is our poor client on his way to Swift's Hospital?' And shall it be said that what is insanity in private life is to be regarded as a rational action when the parties are two countries? It was proposed by Castlereagh and Pitt to equalise the debt by paying off the greater part of the English debt; but how was the equalisation carried out? Why,'by borrowing large sums of money on the account of Ireland.[1]

It requires but a slight acquaintance with the debates in the British Parliament on the question of the Union to perceive how profuse the advocates of that measure were in their expressions of good-will to Ireland. Indeed, it was seriously argued that a Union would amply compensate Ireland for the absenteeism of the landed and educated classes, which was acknowledged on both sides to be a crying evil.

The following circumstance, though slight in itself, will reveal in a different light the real motives of the authors of the Union.

The Archbishop of Armagh (Dr Robinson) had bequeathed a sum of £5000 to trustees to be applied for the purpose of establishing a university at Armagh, provided it should be incorporated within four years after his death. On the 29th July 1799 Lord Cornwallis wrote to the Duke of Portland, stating that if the incorporation did not take place before the 10th October the legacy would lapse, and at the same time enclosing an outline of a plan to be prepared.[2] On the 31st August 1799, the Duke of Portland, writing to Lord Cornwallis

---

[1] "Discussion in the Dublin Corporation on the Repeal of the Union," 1843, pp. 48-49.

[2] "Castlereagh Correspondence," ii. pp. 364, 365.

in reply, makes the following observations "in recommending it to his Excellency to let the legacy lapse":—

"However we should have concurred in wishing that Trinity College had not been placed in Dublin, we are far from being prepared to say that a second university would be of public benefit in Ireland, and more especially in the present circumstance of the impending Union, which no means are so well calculated to perfect and render us indissolubly one nation, as inducements to the better orders of the people of that kingdom to receive a part of their education either at the schools or universities of this country. I should, therefore, very much hesitate as to the policy of enlarging at this moment in Ireland the means of education so far as it regards persons of that description, or in giving any facility to the education of the better classes; and I think it a matter well worthy of consideration in what manner encouragement can be given to Irishmen to study and take degrees in either of the two English universities."[1]

"Will you," said Mr Plunket, speaking against the Union in the Irish House of Commons,—" will you conciliate the mind of the Northern by caricaturing all the defects of the constitution, and then extinguishing it by exhausting his wealth to supply the contributions levied by an Imperial Parliament, and by outraging all his religious and moral feelings by the means which you use to accomplish this abominable project; and will you not by encouraging the drain of absentees, and taking away the influence and example of resident gentlemen, do everything in your power to aggravate the poverty, and to sublimate the ignorance and bigotry of the South."[2]

[1] "Castlereagh Correspondence," ii. pp. 382, 383.
[2] Life of Plunket, i. pp. 146, 147.

CHAPTER II.

THE ADMINISTRATION AND RECALL OF LORD FITZWILLIAM.

By the arrangement of 1782 Ireland obtained a constitution which was theoretically independent. The patriot party both in and out of Parliament strove manfully to render Parliament practically independent by an internal reform and by Catholic emancipation. Mr Grattan in 1797 was constrained to relinquish his attacks on the citadel of corruption, and to yield to forces too powerful for him to resist, by retiring from the Irish Parliament. In his farewell address to the citizens of Dublin, whom he represented, he summed up in one sentence the objects, the hopes, and the struggles of fifteen years. "We moved," he said, "a Reform of Parliament which would give a Constitution to the people, and the Catholic Emancipation which would give a people to the Constitution."

In 1795 the object which Grattan in 1797 relinquished in despair seemed to be within his grasp. "A large section of the Whigs," says Mr Lecky, "in consequence of the French Revolution, had deserted Fox, and had united themselves with Pitt, who, in order to ingratiate himself with his new allies, consented, after very considerable hesitation, to recall Lord Westmoreland, and to send over Lord Fitzwilliam as Lord-Lieutenant. Lord Fitzwilliam was one of the most important personages in the Whig party, an intimate friend of

Grattan, and a warm and avowed supporter of Catholic Emancipation. Such an appointment, at such a moment, could only be construed in Ireland in one way. Catholic Emancipation was the pressing question of the hour. Pitt had early expressed himself in its favour. At a time when it was known to be in agitation, he recalled a Viceroy who was opposed to it, and sent over one who was known to be its ardent friend."[1] He even went further, and solicited a private interview with the arch-agitator himself. "Mr Pitt presents his compliments to Mr Grattan. He wishes much, if it is not disagreeable to Mr Grattan, to have an opportunity of conversing with him confidentially on the subject of an arrangement in Ireland, and for that purpose would take the liberty of requesting to see him, either at four to-day or any time to-morrow morning most convenient to Mr Grattan.—Downing Street, Wednesday, October 15, 1794."[2] Mr Grattan's son gives the following account of this interview, "on the authority of his father, and which there is no reason whatever for thinking inaccurately reported."[3] "At the meeting between Mr Grattan and Mr Pitt, the latter was very plain and very civil in his manner. Mr Grattan stated to him what his party desired, and mentioned the measures that he thought Ireland required; the essential one was the Catholic question. Mr Pitt upon this remarked, 'Ireland has already got much.' Mr Grattan did not tell him how she had got it.[4] They did not enter into the details of

[1] "Leaders of Public Opinion," pp. 142, 143.
[2] "Life of the Right Hon. Henry Grattan," by his son Henry Grattan, Esq., M.P., iv. p. 175. Mr Lecky thinks this work to be "probably the best history of Ireland at the period under consideration."—"Leaders of Public Opinion," p. 139.
[3] "Leaders of Public Opinion in Ireland," p. 143.
[4] The Editor thus explains, "By her armed volunteers."

the Catholic question, but Mr Grattan put it down upon paper, in reply to which Mr Pitt used these words, 'Not to bring it forward as a Government measure, but if Government were pressed, to YIELD IT.' This, unquestionably was a concession of the Catholic question; for Mr Pitt knew well that the question would be pressed; it was certain to be brought on. All parties—Protestant, Presbyterian, and Catholic—had called for it, and at their meetings passed resolutions in its support. Nothing could keep it back; it was not an opposition question, nor did it stand in need of any instigation; and of this Mr Pitt was well aware. This was the arrangement he made with Mr Grattan, and as the latter often mentioned, 'such were the identical expressions.'"[1] Lord Fitzwilliam's account of the circumstances under which he assumed the Viceroyalty, and his instructions from the Cabinet, confirms the accuracy of Mr Grattan's report of the "Carnarvon Conversation" of the eighteenth century. The following statement was made by Lord Fitzwilliam in the English House of Lords on the 19th March 1799. It is placed in the report in inverted commas, and was evidently furnished to the reporter verbatim as his Lordship's authorised and well considered explanation. "I have understood that it has been stated in another place that, during my administration in Ireland, I was never required to retract what I had been directed by Government to propose. If it has been stated that I never received orders to bring forward the question of Catholic Emancipation on the part of the Government, I admit that statement to be true. But in justification of the part I took at the

[1] "Life of Right Hon. Henry Grattan," by his son Henry Grattan, Esq., M.P., iv. p. 177. Mr Grattan had been warned by Mr Serjeant Adair of Mr Pitt's duplicity, and had been advised to reduce to writing, in Mr Pitt's presence, the terms of the arrangement; that otherwise Mr Pitt would cheat him.—*Ibid*, pp. 176, 177.

period, and in my conscience I believe the events that occurred have led to the evils that now exist, and have stamped the doom of that ill-fated country, it is necessary to these statements I should add a short history of the transaction. Yielding to the argument of not wishing to entangle Government in difficulties upon the subject at that period, I admit that under orders clearly understood by me, not to give rise to or bring forward the question of Catholic Emancipation, on the part of the Government I assumed the government of Ireland. But in yielding to this argument I entered my protest against resisting the question if it should be brought forward from any other quarter, and I made most distinct declarations that in case of its being brought forward it should receive my full support. With these declarations I assumed the government of Ireland. This I state upon my honour. I should not have introduced it had I not deemed it necessary to give this explanation."[1]

On the 4th of January 1795 Lord Fitzwilliam arrived in Dublin. At a meeting of the Cabinet on the 19th March 1795, it was unanimously determined to recall him, "as a measure necessary for the preservation (or as we would say, 'for the integrity') of the Empire." Mr Lecky thus describes this three months' Viceroyalty—"Petitions in unprecedented numbers poured in from the Catholics, asking for emancipation; and the great majority of the Protestants were unquestionably strongly in favour of it. Lord Fitzwilliam was afterwards able to represent to the king the unusual approbation with

---

[1] "Parliamentary Register," viii. pp. 276, 277. Lord Grenville, in reply, was only able to state he had no recollection nor knowledge of any such protest. He did not attempt to contradict Lord Fitzwilliam's solemn statement upon his honour.—*Ibid*, p. 277.

which the emancipation of the Catholics was received on the part of his Protestant subjects; and in his letter to Lord Carlisle after his recall he described the state of feeling in Ireland in terms which need no comment.[1] It was a time, he wrote, when the jealousy and alarm which certainly at the first pervaded the minds of the Protestant body exist no longer—when not one Protestant corporation, scarcely an individual, has come forward to deprecate and oppose the indulgence claimed by the higher order of Catholics—when even some of those who were most alarmed in 1793, and were then the most violent opposers, declare the indulgences now asked to be only the necessary consequences of those granted at that time, and positively essential to secure the well-being of the two countries.[2] Lord Fitzwilliam, in answering the addresses that were presented to him, used language which clearly intimated his sympathy with their cause, and such language coming at such a time from the representative of the Sovereign, very naturally removed all doubts from the minds of the Catholics. In Parliament the almost universal feeling of the country was fully reflected. As on the occasion of Irish Emancipation in 1782, extraordinary supplies were voted in testimony of the loyalty of the nation. Grattan, though without an official position, became virtually the leader of the Government, and the French party appeared to have almost disappeared. Grattan obtained leave to bring in an Emancipation Bill with but three dissentient voices, and that Bill had been drawn up by him in concert

---

[1] Lord Fitzwilliam's letters to Lord Carlisle are recorded in "Parliamentary Debates," xlii. pp. 431-447.

[2] In 1793, Roman Catholics in Ireland were admitted to the elective franchise, but the privilege of sitting in Parliament was still withheld.

with Lord Fitzwilliam and the Cabinet. It was understood that a Reform Bill would follow; and one of the most important leaders of the United Irishmen afterwards said, that in that case their quarrel with England was at an end. The whole Catholic population were strung to the highest pitch of excitement. The Protestants were for the most part enthusiastically loyal, and the revolutionary spirit had almost subsided when Pitt suddenly and peremptorily recalled Lord Fitzwilliam, and made the rebellion which followed inevitable."[1] Lord Fitzwilliam had, as appears by his letters, duly informed the British Cabinet of every step he had taken. The Irish Parliament had met on the 22d January. From the 8th January, when he first wrote to the Cabinet on the Catholic question, till the 8th February, when it was first objected to, Lord Fitzwilliam had no reason to believe he was not acting in strict conformity with the views of the English Government. They did not even hint an objection till the Emancipation Bill had been presented in Parliament as a Government measure, and till the hopes of the Irish Catholic population were raised to the highest at the immediate prospect of relief from galling disabilities. Writing to the Duke of Portland, Lord Fitzwilliam refused to be the person to raise a flame in the country that nothing short of arms could keep down, and left him to determine whether if he was not to be supported he ought not to be removed.[2]

Several minor motives, such as the dismissal of Mr Beresford and Mr Cooke from their offices, have been given for Lord Fitzwilliam's recall. "But," says Mr Lecky, "besides these reasons it is probable that he

[1] "Leaders of Public Opinion in Ireland," pp. 143-145.
[2] "Grattan's Life," iv. pp. 182-194.

(Mr Pitt) was already looking forward to the Union.[1] The steady object of his later Irish policy was to corrupt and to degrade, in order that he ultimately might destroy the Legislature of the country. Had Parliament been made a mirror of the national will—had the Catholics been brought within the pale of the Constitution—his policy would have been defeated."[2]

On his recall Lord Fitzwilliam demanded, in the House of Lords, an investigation of the circumstances under which he was deprived of his position as Lord-Lieutenant. The Government, of course, declined to accede to the application. The dismissal was a matter of indignant comment in the Parliaments of both countries. In the Irish House of Commons, on the 2d March 1795, Sir Lawrence Parsons said—"If the Cabinet

---

[1] The records of the State Paper Office confirm Mr Lecky's surmise. Thus, on March 30, 1795, Mr Pelham, the Irish Secretary, writes to the Duke of Portland with respect to Lord Fitzwilliam's correspondence with Lord Carlisle, to which I have alluded—the letter being marked "secret." "The letters were distributed among Lord Fitzwilliam's friends, and are now in general circulation. One passage is much talked of here (in Dublin). It is a quotation from a confidential despatch from your Grace, in which you say that deferring this question would be the means of doing a greater service to the British Empire than it has been capable of receiving since the Revolution. The construction put upon these words by many people (though falsely in my opinion) is that the intention of Ministers was to keep the Catholic question alive and in suspense till a peace, and then employ it as a means of forming a Union between the two countries."—Froude's " English in Ireland," iii. p. 163, note. In a letter from the Duke of Portland to Lord Camden, the Lord-Lieutenant, dated April 13, 1795, and marked " Private and secret," " The Duke said he was prepared for the construction which would be placed upon his words. The Secretary (Mr Pelham) must neither avow nor disavow it. The private correspondence between men in public employment ought to be kept religiously secret, and Mr Pelham was not to allow himself to be betrayed into explanations. He was rather to enter his solemn protest once for all against any reference to information of so delicate and sacred a nature."—Froude's " English in Ireland," iii. p. 166, note.

[2] "Leaders of Public Opinion," p. 146.

of Great Britain had held out an assent to the Catholic question, and had afterwards retracted, it was an insult to the nation which the House should resent." "It now appeared that the country had been duped, that nothing was to be done for the people."[1]

On the 21st April 1795, Mr Grattan stated "that Catholic Emancipation was not only the concession of the British Cabinet, but its precise engagement." "My friends," he said, "declared that they would never support any Government that would resist that bill, and it was agreed to by that quarter with perfect concurrence."[2]

On the 31st January 1799, in the English House of Commons, Mr Sheridan, speaking against the Union, adverted "to the shameful manner in which Lord Fitzwilliam was recalled from Ireland at a moment when he was supposed to have been sent over to grant to the Roman Catholics the rights and privileges which they claimed. The cup of concession was just presented to their lips, but instead of permitting them to taste of it, it was dashed in their faces." "If he (Mr Pitt) is acquainted, as surely he is, with the workings of the human heart, must he not be well aware of what men will do when so provoked?"[3]

Again, on February 11, 1799, Mr Sheridan said—"The

[1] "Grattan's Life," iv. p. 188. Sir L. Parsons, in the same speech, used the following words:—"If the Irish Administration has encouraged the Catholics in their expectations, without the countenance of the British Cabinet, they have much to answer for. If the British Cabinet has assented, and afterwards retracted, the demon of darkness could not have done more mischief had he come from hell to throw a firebrand among the people."—"English in Ireland," iii. pp. 156, 157. Sir L. Parsons was not a demagogue. He had represented Trinity College, Dublin, in Parliament. He was father of the third Earl of Rosse, the illustrious astronomer.

[2] "Grattan's Life," iv. 226. [3] "Parliamentary Debates," vii. 667, 668.

natural inference was that when Mr Pitt appeared to countenance the scheme of Emancipation, he never entertained any idea of carrying it into execution, and that he sent over Lord Fitzwilliam merely to dupe the Irish Catholics for a time to suit his own purposes." "The primary object of Lord Fitzwilliam's Administration was, from the first moment of his landing in Ireland, avowed to be the complete emancipation of the Catholics. It was known by every member of the Irish Parliament, and to every man in the country it was equally well known, that it constituted the avowed ground of Lord Fitzwilliam's recall, and yet so far was it from exciting their displeasure, that there never was a Lord-Lieutenant who left Ireland accompanied with testimonies of more general regret for his departure than Lord Fitzwilliam."[1] Again, "Mr Pitt had argued it was unsafe to grant Catholic Emancipation without Union. He (Mr Sheridan) would then ask why he had authorised Lord Fitzwilliam to promise it, why he had raised that expectation in the minds of the Catholics, of the fallacy of which he had since endeavoured to convince them by a system of cruel massacre and torture of every denomination? He would repeat it, that he considered the right honourable gentleman, and those who supported him with a mercenary confidence, as the authors of all the calamities which had befallen that unhappy country."[2]

Speaking in the English House of Commons on 21st April 1800, Mr (Lord) Grey said, "Lord Fitzwilliam was recalled, and there then began a system of tyranny,

---

[1] "Parliamentary Register," viii. p. 5. Had Mr Sheridan lived to witness the departure of Lord and Lady Aberdeen from Ireland on August 3, 1886, he would have gladly modified this opinion.

[2] "Parliamentary Register," viii. p. 9.

cruelty, and barbarity which continues to the present time."[1]

"Mr Pitt," says Grattan's biographer, "abandoned his principles, his promises, and his professions. He first deceived and then recalled Lord Fitzwilliam, and committed the basest breach of public faith that had occurred since the days of Lord Strafford, and not very dissimilar from it. By so doing he gave the country over to the United Irishmen, and prepared the way for the Insurrection and the Union. His measures were fatal for British character, and the Irish people henceforth lost all confidence in the British Government."[2]

"It is certain," says Mr Lecky, "that the recall of Lord Fitzwilliam arrested a policy which would have made the Union at that time impossible. By raising the hopes of the Catholics almost to certainty, and then dashing them to the ground; by taking this step at the very moment when the inflammatory spirit engendered by the Revolution had begun to spread among the people, Pitt sowed in Ireland the seeds of discord and bloodshed, of religious animosities and social disorganisation, which paralysed the energies of the country, and rendered possible the success of his machinations. The rebellion of 1798, with all the accumulated miseries it entailed, was the direct and predicted consequence of his policy."[3]

[1] Woodfall's "Parliamentary Reports," ii. 403.
[2] "Grattan's Life," iv. p. 195. Grattan declared that in recalling Fitzwilliam "Britain had planted a dagger in Ireland's heart."—"English in Ireland," iii. p. 156.
[3] "Leaders of Public Opinion," pp. 146, 147.

CHAPTER III.

A SYSTEM OF HORRORS.

"CONSIDERING," says Mr Lecky, "the past history of the country, and the inflammatory elements that were abroad in Europe, Ireland in 1795 was singularly easy to govern, had it been governed honestly and by honest men. But it was not in human nature that the loyalty of the Catholics should survive the Administration of Lord Fitzwilliam. Their hopes had been raised to the highest point; the language and demeanour of the representative of the Sovereign had been equivalent to a pledge that they would be relieved of their disqualifications; they could point with pride to their perfect loyalty for the space of a hundred years, in spite of the penal laws, of the rebellions of 1715 and of 1745, and of the revolt of the colonies; they had won to their cause the immense majority of their fellow-countrymen, and had advanced to the very threshold of the Constitution when the English Minister interposed to blight their prospects, and exerted all the influence of the Government against them."[1]

Lord Camden succeeded Lord Fitzwilliam in the Viceroyalty. His Secretary, Mr Pelham, speaking in the Irish House of Commons on the first night of his official appearance in that Assembly, thus summarily disposed of the Catholic question. " He stated," says

[1] Lecky's "Leaders of Public Opinion," p. 149.

the editor of the "Castlereagh Correspondence," "with great heat and emphasis, that 'concessions to the Catholics seemed only to increase their demands; that what they now sought was incompatible with the existence of a Protestant Constitution; that concession must stop somewhere; it had already reached the utmost limit—it could not be allowed to proceed—and here he would plant his foot, and never consent to recede an inch farther.'"

"The debate was continued during the night and until eight in the morning, with the most unusual warmth and eloquence, and the question was lost. From that moment the popular feeling with its desperate decision and a system of horrors commenced, and Mr Pelham returned in disgust to England."[1]

Mr Lecky recommends to the public the study "of the clear and evidently truthful memoir on the rise and aims of the United Irishmen which was drawn up by their three leaders, O'Connor, Emmet, and MacNevin, when State prisoners."[2] It is to be found in the "Castlereagh Correspondence," and it attributes the spread of revolutionary principles in Ireland to the recall of Lord Fitzwilliam. "Whatever progress," they say, "this United system had made among the Presbyterians of the North, it had, as we apprehend, made but little way among the Catholics throughout the kingdom until after the recall of Earl Fitzwilliam. Notwithstanding many resolutions which had appeared from them, manifesting a growing spirit, they were considered as entertaining not only an habitual progression for monarchy, but as being less attached than the Presbyterians to political liberty. There were, however, certain men

---

[1] "Castlereagh Correspondence," i. pp. 11, 12.
[2] "Leaders of Public Opinion," p. 140.

among them of a different description who rejoiced at the rejection of their claims, because it gave them an opportunity of pointing out that the adversaries of Reform were also their adversaries, and that those two objects could never be separated with any chance of success to either. They used the recall of that nobleman and the rejection of his measures to cement together in political union the Catholic and Presbyterian masses."[1]

Lord Gosford, addressing the magistrates of Armagh in December 1795, gives a concise description of what Lord Londonderry, in editing the correspondence of his brother, Lord Castlereagh, has designated "a system of horrors."[2] The demon of religious animosity was aroused; in the Catholic provinces the recall of Lord Fitzwilliam was the signal for the revival of Defenderism, with its accompanying outrages, while the militant bigotry of the North of Ireland was pressed into the service of the Government, and Ulster was not slow in exhibiting a "vigour beyond the law."

"It is no secret," says Lord Gosford, "that a persecution, accompanied with all the circumstances of ferocious cruelty which have in all ages distinguished the dreadful calamity, is now raging in this country. Neither age nor sex, nor even acknowledged innocence as to any guilt in the late disturbances, is sufficient to excite mercy, much less to afford protection. The only crime which the wretched objects of this ruth-

---

[1] "Castlereagh Correspondence," i. p. 356.

[2] He did not use the expression "system of horrors" unadvisedly. He had experience of that system, having been himself in command of a regiment of cavalry in 1798. See letter of Lord Camden to the Hon. Lieut.-Colonel Stewart (Lord Londonderry), January 11, 1799, "Castlereagh Correspondence," ii. p. 89.

less persecution are charged with, is a crime, indeed, of easy proof; it is simply a profession of the Roman Catholic faith, or an intimate connection with a person professing that faith. A lawless banditti have constituted themselves judges of this new species of delinquency, and the sentence they have pronounced is equally concise and terrible; 'tis nothing less than a confiscation of all property, and an immediate banishment." "These horrors, I say, are now acting, and acting with impunity. The spirit of impartial justice (without which law is nothing better than an instrument of tyranny) has for a time disappeared in this country, and the supineness of the magistracy of Armagh is become a common topic of conversation in every corner of the kingdom."[1]

On the meeting of the Irish Parliament in 1796, Mr Grattan thus described these proceedings in the north of Ireland:—

"He had received the most dreadful accounts; that their object was the extermination of all the Catholics of that country. It was a persecution conceived in the bitterness of bigotry, carried on with the most ferocious barbarity by a banditti who, being of the religion of the State, had committed with the greater audacity and confidence the most horrid murders, and had proceeded from robbery and massacre to extermination. They had repealed by their own authority all the laws lately passed in favour of the Catholics, had established in place of those laws the inquisition of a mob resembling Lord George Gordon's fanatics, equalling them in outrage and surpassing them far in perseverance and success.

"Their modes of outrage were as various as they

[1] "Grattan's Life," iv. pp. 233, 234.

were atrocious; they sometimes forced by terror the masters of families to dismiss their Catholic servants; they sometimes forced landlords by terrors to dismiss their Catholic tenantry; they seized as deserters numbers of Catholic weavers, sent them to the county gaol, transmitted them to Dublin, where they remained in close prison, until some lawyers from compassion pleaded their cause and procured their enlargement, nothing appearing against them of any kind whatsoever. Those insurgents called themselves Orange Boys or Protestant Boys—that is, a banditti of marauders committing massacre in the name of God, and exercising despotic power in the name of liberty."[1] "They had very generally given the Catholics notice to quit their farms and dwellings, which notice is plastered on their houses, and conceived in these short but plain words—'Go to Hell, Connaught will not receive you—fire and faggot.—Will. Thresham and John Thrustout.'" "I collect that the Catholic inhabitants of Armagh have been actually put out of the protection of the law; that the magistrates have been supine or partial, and that the horrid banditti has met with complete success, and from the magistracy with very little discouragement."[2] These services were recognised by others beside the Government, whom they helped to carry the Union. "To the Armagh persecution," says the "Memoir of the State Prisoners," "is the Union of United Irishmen most exceedingly indebted. The persons and properties of the wretched Catholics of that county were exposed to the merciless attacks of an Orange faction which was certainly in many in-

---

[1] "Grattan's Life," iv. pp. 237, 238.
[2] *Ibid.*, iv. pp. 238, 239. Mr Curran stated in the Irish House of Commons that "1400 Catholic families had been expelled from their homes in Armagh."—Froude's "English in Ireland," iii. p. 195.

stances uncontrolled by the justices of the peace, and claimed to be in all supported by the Government."[1]

Mr Grattan spoke in February 1796. In the same month Theobald Wolfe Tone sailed from America to France for the purpose of pressing on the Government of that country an invasion of Ireland, making use of these occurrences, and more especially the speeches of Lord Clare in opposition to popular rights, "*as his credentials.*"[2]

Thus commenced the "system of horrors," which culminated in the Rebellion of 1798. The further development of that system by the policy of the English Government was described in the British House of Lords by Lord Moira, who afterwards was elevated in the peerage under the title of Marquis of Hastings, and became Governor-General of India. Speaking on the 22nd November 1797, his Lordship said, "Before God and my country, I speak of what I have seen myself. What I have to speak of are not solitary and isolated measures, not partial abuses, but what is adopted as the system of government. I do not talk of a casual system, but of one deliberately determined upon and regularly persevered in. My Lords, I have seen in Ireland the most absurd as well as the most disgusting tyranny that any nation ever groaned under. I have been myself a witness of it in many instances. I have seen it practised and unchecked." . "I have seen in that country a marked distinction made between English and Irish. I have seen troops that have been sent full of this prejudice, that every inhabitant in that kingdom is a rebel to the British Government. I have seen the most wanton

[1] "Castlereagh Correspondence," i. pp. 356, 357.
[2] "Grattan's Life," iv. p. 259.

insults practised upon men of all ranks and conditions. I have seen the most grievous oppression exercised in consequence of a presumption that the person who was the unfortunate object of such oppression was in hostility to the Government, and yet that has been done in a part of the country as quiet and as free from disturbance as the city of London. Who states these things, my Lords, should, I know, be prepared with proofs. I am prepared with them." "There is not one man, my Lords, in Ireland, who is not liable to be taken out of his house at any hour, either of the day or night, to be kept in a rigorous confinement, restricted from all correspondence with the persons who have the management of his affairs, be treated with mixed severity and insult, and yet never know the crime with which he is charged, nor the source from whence the information against him proceeded. I can furnish proofs, my Lords, of many instances in which such cruelty has been exercised upon individuals. I therefore say there is no man who is not exposed to such oppression, and the more so because the constant tone of menace held out, informs him that the very persons who use it may put their threats in practice against him. Your Lordships have hitherto detested the Inquisition. In what did that horrible system differ from the system pursued in Ireland? By the Inquisition a man was liable to be torn from his family and friends, his affairs might be ruined, himself and his children reduced to beggary, yet no crime might be advanced against him to justify the practice of such severity, and if he required to be confronted with his accuser, that first principle of all justice, that right which every man may claim, if, I say, he made this demand, it was denied him, and he was left to groan in prison under the

A System of Horrors.

dreadful uncertainty of the length of his confinement and of his ultimate fate. Such, we are taught to believe, were the horrible practices of the Inquisition. It may be said, between those who distinguish between the system pursued in Ireland and the practices of the Inquisition, that I have forced a comparison, because the torture has not been used in Ireland. What will your Lordships say when I inform you that the torture has been actually practised in the cases of the persons of whom I have been speaking? Men, indeed, have not been put to the rack in Ireland, because that horrible engine was not at hand. But I do know instances of men being picketed, a mode of punishment abolished in this country for some time, on account of its too great severity. I know of men in Ireland being picketed till they fainted. When they recovered, picketed again till they fainted—recovered again, and again picketed till they fainted a third time; and this in order to extort from the tortured sufferers a confession either of their own guilt or the guilt of their neighbours! But I can even go further, men have been half-hanged and then brought to life, in order, by the fear of having that punishment repeated, to induce them to confess the crimes with which they have been charged! Good God, what must the general feeling be in a nation where such measures are adopted. My Lords, I could go much further, but I choose to veil some of the most atrocious parts. These acts which I have stated to your Lordships have been done so publicly that I cannot but consider them as belonging to the system which has been adopted. They have been done in open day, and if you do not hear the recitals of them from the newspapers of Ireland, it is because they are not published from the fear of the publishers being exposed to the vengeance of the Government if they did publish them. I know that authenticated relations of the most oppressive conduct have been refused insertion in the Irish newspapers on this account. The printer says, 'What punishment hangs over me if I do insert them?' What happened to the printers of the *Northern Star?* A party of troops went in broad day and destroyed the whole property, types and everything, belonging to the paper. I enter not now into the nature of the articles inserted in that publication; but surely there were laws sufficient for the punishment of the publishers of that paper, for the criminal code of Ireland is more severe than any I have heard of. The laws, therefore, as I said before, were sufficient for the purpose. But the destruction of the property by the military was done in order to check animadversions in other papers upon the conduct of the Government; because everything is pledged upon the success of this wild and frantic system. Your Lordships have heard of a proclamation, confessedly illegal, requiring the surrender of all arms from a free people. A man reared in an opinion that the Constitution allows every man to keep arms for his defence, and that nothing short of an Act of Parliament can deprive him of that right, might hesitate in bringing in his arms. What is the punishment? It is a contumacy for which there might be some punishment of a moderate nature, however. Yet, what is the recognised and regular punishment in Ireland? A party of the military may go and burn his house and totally destroy his property. I know of instances where this has been practised because the district in which the property has been situated has not brought in such a number of arms as it was conceived were contained in the district." " Do not you see that by such a system you place in the hands of the enemy an engine the most forcible as well as the most fatal? Can anything be more formidable than a statement such as I have laid before you. Upon the accuracy of it, my Lords, it is the dearest wish of my heart to be examined before the Privy Council, or at the bar of this House." " I declare solemnly that I think the moment for conciliation is not past. I think that Ireland may yet be saved, but it can only be by an immediate change of measures." " I wish some little attention to be paid, my Lords, to the conclusion I have drawn. I declare solemnly that if you go on a little longer in the present system, all hope is lost of seeing Ireland connected five years longer with the British Empire. We have tried this system of coercion long enough. I entreat your Lordships, and his Majesty's Ministers, to inform themselves of the effect that has resulted from it. I should be happy, my Lords, to be convinced that during its continuance the numbers of United Irishmen have diminished. But I do assert this not to be the case, and my conviction has been strengthened by intelligence that has been received from the south of Ireland. If this be the fact, would it not be wise and prudent to try another system? I am willing to give all the merit due to the novelty of the measures that have been adopted; the inventive faculties of the authors of them have been extraordinary indeed; they found a throbbing sore, and to allay the pain and irritation they applied a blister to it. That is a true description of the system that has been pursued with respect to Ireland. You say the Irish are insensible of the benefits of the British Constitution, and you withhold all those benefits from them. You goad them with harsh and cruel punishments, and a general infliction and insult are thrown upon the kingdom. I have seen, my Lords, a conquered country held by military force, but never did I see in any conquered country such a tone of insult as has been adopted by Great Britain towards Ireland."[1]

Mr Grattan, in his celebrated letter to his fellow-citizens in 1797, explaining the circumstances of his retirement from Parliament, thus writes:—" It was with a view to restore liberty, and with a view also to secure and immortalise royalty, by restoring to the people self-legislation, we proposed reform—a principle of attraction about which the King and the people would spin on quietly and insensibly in regular movements, and in a system common to them both. 'No, no, no; the half million,' said the Minister, 'that is my principle of attraction.'[2] Among the rich I send my half million, and I despatch my coercion among the people.' His devil went forth; he destroyed liberty and property, he consumed the press, he burned houses and villages, he murdered, and he failed. 'Recall your murderer,' we said, 'and in his place despatch our messenger—try conciliation. You have declared you wish the people should rebel, to which we answer, God forbid; rather let them weary the royal ear with petitions, and let the

[1] "Parliamentary Register," iv. 236-243. Abridged.

[2] This shameful avowal was made in the Irish House of Commons by Lord Clare, when Attorney-General, on the 25th February 1789:—" I recollect Lord Townshend proroguing the Parliament; and I recollect when next they met they voted him an address of thanks, which address cost this nation half a million of money. I hope to God I shall never again see such effects from party. I hope to God I shall never again see half a million of the people's money employed to procure an address from their Representatives. I have ever endeavoured to defend the people, and ever shall oppose measures which may lead to an address which will cost them half-a-million." " Irish Debates," ix. p. 181. Lord Castlereagh during the Union debates used similar language.

A System of Horrors.

dove be again sent to the King, it may bring back the olive; and as to you, thou mad Minister, who pour in regiment after regiment to dragoon the Irish because you have forfeited their affections, we beseech, we supplicate, we admonish; reconcile the people, combat revolution by reform, let blood be your last experiment.'"[1]

"Pray, Mr Emmet," said Lord Clare, the Lord Chancellor, when examining the State prisoners, "what caused the late insurrection?" This was the answer: "The free quarters, the house burnings, the tortures, and the military executions in the counties of Kildare, Carlow, and Wicklow."[2]

[1] "Grattan's Life," iv. 305, 306.
[2] This incident occurred in August 1798.

CHAPTER IV.

THE REBELLION OF 1798 AND THE ENGLISH GOVERNMENT.

AT length "the means taken to make the Rebellion explode"[1] were successful. Into the details of that dreadful episode in history it is not my purpose to enter. I am merely dealing with the Rebellion of 1798 in its relation to the Legislative Union of 1800. Plowden, the Unionist historian, computes the number killed on both sides in this terrible conflict at nearly 70,000. Mr Froude, however, believes this estimate to be exaggerated, although he admits that the insurrection cost many thousand lives.[2] Commenting on the features of the Irish Rebellion, Mr Goldwin Smith says:—" Among the phantoms of hatred and suspicion which arose from this field of carnage was the horrible idea that the English Government had intentionally stimulated the Irish people into rebellion, in order to pave the way for the Union. No evidence in support of this charge can be produced."[3]

From this judgment of Mr Goldwin Smith I am constrained to dissent, for the following reasons :—

1. In November 1797, Lord Carhampton, who had

[1] "Lord Castlereagh's flagitious and (for his reputation) fatal phrase in his examination of Dr MacNevin. This is omitted in the House of Commons Report. Lord Clare told MacNevin they would only print what would serve their purpose."—" Grattan's Life," iv. p. 355.

[2] "English in Ireland," iii. p. 545.

[3] " Irish History and Irish Character," p. 176.

held the post of Commander of the Forces in Ireland since 1795, resigned that position. Sir Jonah Barrington gives this account of the circumstances attending Lord Carhampton's retirement:—"His Lordship had but little military experience, but he was a man of the world, of courage and decision, ardent and obstinate; he determined right or wrong to annihilate the conspiracy. Without the consent of the Irish Government he commanded the troops, that upon all symptoms of insurrectionary movements they should act without waiting for the presence of any civil power. Martial law had not then been proclaimed. He went, therefore, a length that could not possibly be supported; his orders were countermanded by the Lord-Lieutenant (Lord Camden), but he refused to obey the Viceroy, under colour that he had no rank in the army. Lord Carhampton found that the troops in the garrison of Dublin were daily corrupted by the United Irishmen; he therefore withdrew them, and formed two distinct camps on the south and north, some miles from the capital, and thereby, as he conceived, prevented all intercourse of the army with the disaffected of the metropolis. Both measures were disapproved of by the Lord-Lieutenant, whom Lord Carhampton again refused to obey.

"The king's sign-manual was at length procured, ordering him to break up his camps and bring back the garrison; this he obeyed, and marched the troops into Dublin barracks. He then resigned his command, and publicly declared that some deep and insidious scheme of the Minister was in agitation, for instead of suppressing, the Irish Government was obviously disposed to excite an insurrection.[1] Mr Pitt counted on the expert-

[1] Lord Carhampton is better known in England as Colonel Luttrell, the opponent of Wilkes.

ness of the Irish Government to effect a premature explosion. Free quarters¹ were now ordered to irritate the Irish population; slow tortures were inflicted under the pretence of forcing confessions;—the people were goaded and driven to madness.

"General Abercromby, who succeeded as Commander-in-Chief, was not permitted to abate these enormities, and therefore resigned with disgust.² Ireland was by these means reduced to a state of anarchy, and exposed to crime and cruelties to which no nation had ever been subject. The people could no longer bear their miseries. Mr Pitt's object was now effected, and an insurrection was excited."³

Sir Jonah Barrington was a King's Counsel and Judge of the Prerogative Court in Ireland. He had been a member of the Irish Parliament, and an active and eloquent opponent of the Union. The book from which I have quoted was dedicated to his old friend, Mr Plunket, then Lord Plunket, Lord Chancellor of Ireland. Sir Jonah Barrington's account of Lord Carhampton's public declaration was made without fear of contradiction, and has never, so far as I am aware, been challenged.

2. John Scott was successively Attorney-General, Prime-Serjeant, and Chief Justice of Ireland. The

---

¹ "Free quarters," Sir Jonah Barrington adds in a note, "is a term not yet practically known in England. Free quarters rendered officers and soldiers despotic masters of the peasantry, their houses, food, and property, and occasionally their *families*. This measure was resorted to with all its attendant horrors throughout some of the best parts of Ireland previous to the insurrection, and for the purpose of exciting it."

² "On his own responsibility he superseded Lord Camden's orders, and forbade the soldiers to act anywhere, under any circumstances, in suppressing riots, arresting criminals, or in any other function, without the presence and authority of a magistrate."—" English in Ireland," iii. p. 352.

³ "Rise and Fall of the Irish Nation," pp. 350, 351.

last post he held till his death. He was elevated to the peerage under the title of Baron Earlscourt, and subsequently created Earl of Clonmel.

"The following anecdote, which reflects much credit upon his character, was communicated," says Mr Grattan's biographer, "by one of his own relations. Shortly before his death he sent for his nephew, Dean Scott, got him to examine his papers, and destroy those that were useless. There were many relating to politics, that disclosed the conduct of the Irish Government at the period of the disturbances in 1798. There was one letter in particular which fully showed their duplicity, and that they might have crushed the rebellion, but that they let it go on on purpose to carry the Union, and that this was their design. When Lord Clonmel was dying he stated this to Dean Scott,[1] and made him destroy the letter; he further added that he had gone to the Lord-Lieutenant, and told him that, as they knew of the proceedings of the disaffected, it was wrong to permit them to go on; that the Government having it in their power should crush them at once, and prevent the insurrection. He was coldly received, and found that his advice was not relished. That of Lord Clare, Mr Foster, and Bishop Agar had predominated, and in consequence he was not summoned to attend the Privy Council on business of State (his health not being good was advanced as the excuse). On ordinary affairs, however, he still received a summons.

"As an instance of the knowledge the Government

---

[1] "Dean Scott," the biographer adds in a note, "was married to Mr Grattan's niece, and he communicated this statement with the knowledge that it would be made use of in a work of this nature; but he would neither disclose the name of the person who wrote the letter nor more of the contents than above-mentioned."

had of the persons engaged in the Rebellion, Lord Clonmel mentioned this extraordinary circumstance,— that previous to it he had been visited one evening by a person in the middle ranks of life, with whom he was well acquainted. This man told him how much he valued him, and that his life was in danger; that some persons well known to him (the speaker) meant to make him their victim; that as his health was not good a colourable pretence afforded itself of his going off to England with his family; and that if he did not he would be assassinated. Lord Clonmel thanked him, told him he valued his own life very much, but that he valued *his* also, and therefore would wish *him* to go off to England instantly, for that he was suspected and known to Government. The man would not believe it possible. Lord Clonmel told him where he had been, with whom, and what he had been doing on such and such particular nights; that Government knew everything connected with the movements of the conspirators, and that in a short time he would be seized and probably executed. The man was terrified and went off to England the next day. The night after, Government sent to his house to apprehend him, but he was gone. To Lord Clonmel he owed his life.

"Any comment on these extraordinary facts would," says Mr Grattan's biographer, "be superfluous. Posterity will pronounce its sentence, and another more awful tribunal, that which awaits man hereafter."[1]

Mr O'Connell, speaking in his own defence in the State Trials of 1844, read the passage I have quoted in his address to the jury.

---

[1] "Grattan's Life," ii. pp. 145-147. Mr Grattan's biographer refers to these circumstances in another part of his work and says—" This attaches a heavy charge against the Irish ministers and affixes to their memories a disgrace that is indelible."—" Grattan's Life," iv. 349.

3. In the discussion on Repeal of the Union in the Dublin Corporation in 1843, Mr O'Connell made the following statement. He spoke to the same effect in the Repeal Debate in the House of Commons in 1834, and also on his trial in 1844.

"What was the state of Ireland when the Union was accomplished? A rebellion was fomented; an insurrectionary movement was encouraged; the traitors to the Crown had been permitted to ripen and bring their treason to maturity. Let no man tell me it is not so. I have the authority of Bushè and Plunket that it was so; and what I set a higher value on, because it is more decisive, I have the evidence which comes out of the hands of the then existing Government. The Irish House of Commons in 1798 had a secret committee to inquire into the facts and circumstances connected with the Rebellion. The report of that committee was published, and I take my authority from it. I say the Irish Government cherished and fomented treason at that dreadful period, and allowed the traitors to go at large with impunity for a time, in order that the treason might ripen into an extinguishable rebellion. That is a serious charge made by me. I made it before, and I will tell you the evidence to support it. My Lord, I find that treason was first hatched in Ulster; that an armed organisation was first commenced in that province, and was there alone successful to any extent. A meeting of nine colonels of United Irishmen took place once a fortnight in the town of Ballynahinch, in the county Down, a place where a battle was fought afterwards. One of these colonels was found to be a double traitor—his name was Maguan; had not only that military rank, but was also a member of the County Down Directory, and besides, of the Ulster

Chief Directory. He was a double-dyed traitor in not only holding these military and civil offices in the treasonable Union, but also by being a spy for the Government, receiving bribes for the purpose of communicating intelligence to the Rev. Dr Clelland, a Protestant divine, who was a magistrate in that district. This clergyman also acted as land-agent to Lord Londonderry, father of Lord Castlereagh. That traitor Maguan began his communications on the 14th of April 1797, and at every meeting of the colonels held he forwarded an account of the proceedings, and a list of the persons in attendance, to the Rev. Dr Clelland, who forwarded them to the Castle. He also sent a full account of all the proceedings, as well of the meetings of colonels as of the county and provincial committees, to the reverend gentleman, who regularly forwarded them to the Castle. He continued giving this information down to the latter end of May 1798. The Government could in the meantime have laid hold of all the colonels, and also the members of the committees, if they chose to do so. They could have apprehended his eight military companions, captains, committee-men, and others of the parties, and they could have put an end to the conspiracy. Why did they not do it? It was their solemn duty to do so. In ordinary times they would have apprehended them all at once, and executed every man of them; and had it been done in that case much human blood would have been spared which afterwards unhappily deluged the land.

"The country was obviously weakened by the Rebellion for the purpose of passing the Union, but they pulled the cord a little too tight and too long, for if other counties were driven to madness as Wexford had been, that which was unfortunately a bloody Rebellion would have been still more unfortunately a sanguinary revolution. What a horrible crime the rulers of that day committed. Can any one deny the fact? If so, I have the evidence of Nicholas Maguan, the colonel of the United Irishmen I have alluded to, who was a member of the provincial and county committees, and I have the testimony of Lord (then Mr) Plunket, who accused Castlereagh of fomenting the embers of a lingering rebellion, of hallooing the Protestant against the Catholic and the Catholic against the Protestant, of artfully keeping alive domestic dissensions for the purposes of subjugation. The evidence relative to Maguan before the Secret Committee will be found in the appendix, No. 14, to that report. Here, my Lord, is Bushe's description of that same spirit, and although I do not call it a confirmation of the passage I have read, I do so because it does not require any confirmation, and it cannot deceive us.—' The basest corruption and artifice,' he says, 'were excited to promote the Union. All the worst passions of the human heart were entered in the service, and all the most depraved ingenuity of the human intellect tortured to devise new contrivances for fraud.' "[1]

[1] "Debate in the Dublin Corporation on the Repeal of the Union," 1843, p. 38.

CHAPTER V.

MILITARY FORCE AND THE UNION.

THE Legislative Union between England and Ireland was first proposed in the Irish House of Commons on the 22nd January 1799. It was on that occasion rejected. The measure ultimately received the royal assent on the 1st of August 1800, and came into operation on the 1st January 1801.

Having regard to these dates, the following extracts, taken from the correspondence of Lords Cornwallis and Castlereagh, and containing admissions that the presence of English troops in the country was necessary to carry the measure, will be of interest. On the 14th January 1801, when the struggle was over, Lord Cornwallis, writing to Lord Castlereagh, pays to the Rebellion of 1798 the remarkable tribute of having "assisted the Union. Timid men will not venture on any change of system, however wise and just, unless their fears are alarmed by pressing dangers."[1]

It was in fact necessary to the success of the Union, that Ireland should be deprived of self-reliance and of self-help.

On the 7th September 1798 Lord Castlereagh informs Mr Pitt in a letter marked *private;* "The force that

---

[1] "If Mr Pitt is firm he will meet with no difficulty, and the misfortunes of the present times are much in his favour, on the same grounds that the Rebellion assisted the Union," &c. "Cornwallis Correspondence," iii. pp. 331, 332. The allusion seems to be to the Catholic question.

will be disposable when the troops from England arrive, cannot fail to dissipate every alarm, and I consider it peculiarly advantageous that we shall owe our security so entirely to the interposition of Great Britain. I have always been apprehensive of that false confidence which might arise from an impression that security had been obtained by our own exertions. Nothing would tend so much to make the public mind impracticable with a view to that future settlement, without which we can never hope for any permanent tranquillity." [1]

The presence of British troops for the purpose of impressing the people of Ireland with the idea that they were unable to protect themselves, was objectionable. Such a design was, however, praiseworthy as compared with the plan of filling the country with British soldiery for the purpose of carrying the Union by force and terrorism. When the regiments of English militia, who considered that they offered their services for the emergency of the Rebellion, and not for the general defence of Ireland, manifested an anxiety at the close of that Rebellion to return to their homes, Lord Castlereagh, in a letter, dated 22nd November 1798, to Mr Wickham, to be laid before the Duke of Portland, thus deprecated their withdrawal—" The alarming effect of withdrawing from this country, where the treason is rather quiescent than abandoned, the flower of its army at a period when the King's Ministers have in contemplation a great constitutional settlement, his Grace (Portland) will feel. The Lord-Lieutenant's opinion decidedly is that without the force in question it would expose the King's

[1] "Castlereagh Correspondence," i. p. 337. Mr Parnell, in a recent speech in Parliament, expressed his desire that the Irish people should realise the advantages of self-help. Lord Castlereagh, who wished to degrade that people, was naturally anxious to dissipate all idea of self-reliance from their minds.

interest in this kingdom to hazard a measure which, however valuable in its future efforts, cannot fail in the discussion very seriously to agitate the public mind, and upon which the well-disposed members of the community may be expected warmly to be opposed to each other." In a postscript, Lord Castlereagh states that he had communicated with Lord Buckingham, and that "his Lordship saw the importance of their (the militia regiments') services in the same point of view with the Lord-Lieutenant; he went so far as to say, that in his Lordship's judgment, the event of the question of the Union is altogether dependent on their continuance."[1] Lord Cornwallis, writing directly to the Duke of Portland on 15th December 1798, says, "The necessity of keeping a considerable number of British troops here is obvious, and I should recommend that every means might be taken to induce some regiments of English militia to relieve those which are now serving in Ireland."[2] Lord Cornwallis applied, as we have seen, for British troops. The Duke of Portland proposed some time afterwards to place 5000 Russians at his disposal.[3] Lord Cornwallis, to his honour be it said, declined the offer. "If," he replies, "the Russians were to be sent over to us, their soldiers would be told they were going to a country that was in a state of rebellion, and if any parties of them should be called upon to support some of our loyal, but, in my opinion, indiscreet magistrates, who see no remedy for our evils but that of scouring the country and hunting down rebels (forgetful that they are creating more than they can possibly destroy), these

---

[1] "Castlereagh Correspondence," ii. pp. 13, 14.
[2] "Cornwallis Correspondence," "Secret and Confidential," iii. p 19.
[3] Portland to Cornwallis, October 14, 1799. "Most Secret and Confidential." "Cornwallis Correspondence," iii. 137.

troops, unacquainted with our language and with the nature of our Government, would give a loose to their natural ferocity, and a scene of indiscriminate plunder and murder must ensue."[1] Lord Cornwallis was kindly and humane, and had the instincts of a gentleman; he was unworthy of the work in which the force of circumstances placed him, and which entailed on him the loss of all self-esteem. On the 21st January 1800, in a "private" letter to the Duke of Portland, Lord Cornwallis writes—"The most seditious and artful handbills are now in general circulation, calling upon the yeomanry, Orangemen, and Catholics to form one solid and indissoluble bond of opposition to the Union; and one of these productions is peculiarly addressed to the passions of the yeomanry, by stating that no Government can wrest the Parliament from 60,000 armed and tried men. These circumstances strongly confirm the expediency of hastening the departure of the forces which are destined to serve in this country, and it might not have a bad effect if one or two of the regiments were to pass from Liverpool to Dublin," &c.[2]

The yeomanry were serviceable for goading the people into rebellion by burnings, robberies, murders, and other outrages too horrible to mention. When, however, the British Government were compassing the destruction of the Irish Parliament and the degradation of Irishmen—Catholic and Protestant alike—it was feared the strain would be too severe even for their well-tried

---

[1] October 19, 1799. "Most Secret and Confidential." "Cornwallis Correspondence," iii. 137, 138. He also stated the presence of these troops would countenance the suggestion "that the Union was to be forced upon this kingdom by the terror and the bayonets of barbarians."

[2] "Cornwallis Correspondence," iii. 168. See Castlereagh's letter, marked "Private," January 20, 1800, to Portland. "Cornwallis Correspondence," iii. 166, 167.

loyalty. The editor of the "Castlereagh Correspondence" tells us that "the Parliament of Ireland met on the 15th January 1800. Though in the speech delivered from the throne by Lord Cornwallis there was no allusion to the Union, it was well known that the measure would be revived and urged with all the influence that Government possessed. In the debate which ensued upon the address, Sir Lawrence Parsons, after a strong speech against a Union, moved an amendment to assure his Majesty that Ireland was already inseparably united with Great Britain, but that his Irish subjects were too sensible of the blessings which they enjoyed from the exertions of an independent resident Parliament not to feel themselves bound at all times, and peculiarly at that moment, to maintain it. This amendment, supported by Mr Plunket, the late Prime-Serjeant Fitzgerald,[1] Mr Grattan, Arthur Moore, Charles Bushe, and others, was rejected by a majority of 138 to 96. On the breaking up of the House a riot took place in the streets, and some of the advocates of the Union were insulted by the populace. The Government was not backward in providing the means of repressing any seditious demonstrations which the opponents of Union might excite; and on the 21st January[2] the Commons, on the motion of Lord Castlereagh, voted that 10,000 men of the Irish Militia should be allowed to volunteer into the line at a bounty of six to ten guineas per man; and it was afterwards determined that their place in Ireland should be supplied by English Militia regiments."[3]

---

[1] This gentleman had been dismissed from his high office for opposing the Union.

[2] The date of Lord Cornwallis' letter to the Duke of Portland.

[3] "Castlereagh Correspondence," iii. pp. 210, 211. "This," says Mr Butt, "appeared to be an act influenced only by the desire to invite Irish

We learn from Lord Cornwallis, on 31st January 1800, that "the clamour against the Union is increasing rapidly, and every degree of violence is to be expected. As none of the English regiments have yet arrived, I have been under the necessity of ordering the Lancashire Volunteers (Lord Grey de Wilton's) from Youghal to Dublin; this will create much alarm and abuse, but the apprehensions of our friends rendered the measure absolutely necessary." [1]

As the measure of the Union advanced, the advantage of having English troops in Ireland was more keenly felt. Thus Mr Cooke, in a "secret" letter from London, dated 5th April 1800, cheers Lord Castlereagh by this significant announcement, "The 2000 Guards will be in Ireland by the 1st of May." [2] Thus, too, the same gentlemen writes to Lord Cornwallis on 28th April 1800, " The Duke of Portland has desired me to state to your Excellency that the brigade of Guards shall be sent, and *whatever troops* (*sic*) you may require." [3]

A statement of the army payments in Ireland for five years ended January 1801 was compiled by Mr Staunton in 1843 from " Reports of Session, 1830, No. 667." "It will be seen," he says, "that they increased even after the Rebellion was completely suppressed to the last sitting of the Irish Parliament. All these payments

valour to the defence of the Empire in its foreign wars; but mark what followed. Ten regiments of the Irish Militia accepted the bounty and volunteered for foreign service. They were instantly replaced by ten English regiments; so that it was manifest it was not for the purpose of taking troops abroad that this was done. While England was engaged in a desperate continental struggle Ireland was held by 130,000 armed men —troops that had free quarters on the people, and on whose use of that privilege I do not choose to dwell." "Proceedings of the Home Rule Conference," 1873, p. 20.

[1] Cornwallis to Ross. "Cornwallis Correspondence," iii. p. 175.
[2] "Castlereagh Correspondence," iii. p. 261.   [3] *Ibid.*, iii. p. 292.

were charged to Ireland exclusively, and they were the principal cause of the accumulation of the debt—comparatively small as it was—due by Ireland at the period of the Union.

Year.	Army Expenditure.
1797,	£2,221,505
1798,	2,548,331
1799,	3,697,314
1800,	3,879,569
1801,	4,285,362

"The military force was never after so large in Ireland as in the year ended the 5th of January 1801, which was the time the Act of Union became operative. In the year after the expenditure fell to £3,505,338, and in the succeeding year to £2,876,621. It advanced a little in 1804, and considerably in 1805, but it never was so high as in the year ended 5th January 1801."[1]

"There is something," says Mr O'Connell, "which bespeaks a foregone conclusion when we look to the military force in Ireland. In 1797, when Ireland was threatened with a rebellion, the military force was but 78,995; in 1798, when a rebellion actually raged, it was 91,995; in 1799, after the rebellion was over, it was 114,052; and in 1800, two years after the rebellion, when the Union was carried, it increased to 129,258 soldiers, or what Lord Strafford called 'good lookers-on.'"[2]

"It is not possible," said Mr Sheridan in the English House of Commons, "that in the present state of Ireland the people can declare and act upon their genuine sentiments; and let any man who has a head to con-

---

[1] "Prize Essays on Repeal of the Union," pp. 40, 41.
[2] "Debate in Dublin Corporation on Repeal of the Union, 1843," p. 43.

ceive and a heart to feel for the miseries of Ireland, put this memorable question to himself: 'Is it possible that the fair and unbiassed sense of the people of Ireland can be collected at this time on this question?' The English force in that country is at once an answer to this question."[1]

[1] January 23, 1799. "Parliamentary Debates," vii. p. 586.

CHAPTER VI.

ROBBERY, TORTURE, MURDER, AND THE UNION.

IF the conduct of the troops serving in Ireland had been regulated by the strictest discipline, their numbers, coupled with the determination of the Government to carry the Union despite of all opposition, would have rendered their presence a source of terror and of intimidation. "Nothing," writes Lord Castlereagh to the Duke of Portland, January 2, 1799, "but an established conviction that the English Government will never lose sight of the Union till it is carried can give the measure a chance of success. The friends of the question look with great anxiety for Mr Pitt's statement; it is not only of the last importance, from the ability with which the subject will be handled, but from the opportunity it will afford him of announcing to this country (Ireland) the determined purpose of Government in both countries, to be discouraged neither by defeat nor difficulty, but to agitate the question again and again till it succeeds. This principle is the foundation of our strength, and cannot be too strongly impressed on this side of the water."[1] "This object (the Union), will now be urged to the utmost, and will, even in the case, if it should happen, of any present failure, be renewed on every occasion until it succeeds."[2]

[1] "Castlereagh Correspondence," ii. pp. 81, 82.
[2] "Cornwallis Correspondence," iii. 20, December 21, 1798.

To a Government with this policy the mighty armament then in Ireland was meant for something more than mere parade.

Lord Cornwallis, indeed, had deprecated the idea of sending Russian troops into the country. The army in Ireland, however, from 1798 till 1800, rivalled in ferocity the semi-civilised Muscovite hordes.

Lord Cornwallis was appointed to the Viceroyalty as a military Lord-Lieutenant. He came to Ireland on June 20, 1798, the day before the great engagement at Vinegar Hill, in the county of Wexford, which was the crisis of the Rebellion. His extensive experience in India and America had rendered him familiar with scenes of horror and of carnage. This is the estimate that the veteran soldier formed of the troops serving under his command in Ireland.

Writing a few days after his arrival in Dublin to the Duke of Portland a "private" letter, Lord Cornwallis makes the following observations:—" The accounts that you see of the numbers of the enemy destroyed in every action are, I conclude, greatly exaggerated; from my own knowledge of military affairs I am sure that a very small proportion of them only could be killed in battle, and I am much afraid that any man in a brown coat who is found within several miles of the field of action is butchered without discrimination. It shall be one of my first objects to soften the ferocity of our troops, which, I am afraid, in the Irish corps at least, is not confined to the private soldiers."[1] Again:—" The violence of our friends, and their folly in endeavouring to make it a religious war, added to the ferocity of our troops who delight in murder, most powerfully counter-

[1] June 28, 1798, " Cornwallis Correspondence," ii. p. 355.

act all plans of conciliation."[1] In a "private and confidential" letter to the Duke of Portland, Lord Cornwallis says:—"The Irish Militia are totally without discipline, contemptible before the enemy when any serious resistance is made to them, but ferocious and cruel in the extreme when any poor wretches, either with or without arms, come within their power; in short, murder appears to be their favourite pastime."[2]

As illustrating the "delight" of the soldiery "in murder—their favourite pastime," I may mention a circumstance related by Lord Cloncurry. Having given some account of a Mr Wogan Browne, a gentleman of property and position in the county Kildare, with whom he was on terms of intimacy, his Lordship proceeds:— "Another occurrence in the history of Wogan Browne shows how precarious was the hold which in those days such a man enjoyed of his life. He was in the same year, '98, seized as a rebel in the street of Naas, his county town, by some hostile soldiers, and a rope placed about his neck for the purpose of hanging him, when the accidental arrival of a dragoon with a letter addressed to him by the Lord-Lieutenant on public business interrupted his captors in their work of murder."[3]

In his letters to his life-long correspondent, Major-General Ross, the father of the editor of his "Correspondence," Lord Cornwallis speaks still more plainly than in his communications with the English Cabinet. After a reference to the martial law by which the country was governed, he says:—"But all this is trifling compared to the numberless murders that are hourly committed by our people without any process or ex-

---

[1] Cornwallis to Ross, July 1, 1798. "Cornwallis Correspondence," ii. p. 355.

[2] July 8, 1798. "Cornwallis Correspondence," ii. p. 357.

[3] "Personal Recollections of Valentine Lord Cloncurry," p. 178.

amination whatever. The yeomanry are in the style of the Loyalists of America, only much more numerous and powerful, and a thousand times more ferocious. These men have saved the country, but they now take the lead in rapine and murder. The Irish militia with few officers, and those chiefly of the worst kind, follow closely on the heels of the yeomanry in murder and every kind of atrocity, and the Fencibles take a share, although much behind-hand with the others." "The conversation of the principal persons of the country tends to encourage this system of blood; and the conversation even at my table, where you will suppose I do all I can to prevent it, always turns on hanging, shooting, burning, &c., &c.; and if a priest has been put to death, the greatest joy is expressed by the whole company. So much for Ireland and my wretched situation."[1]

On August 31, 1798, Lord Cornwallis issued a general order, in which he says:—"It is with very great concern that Lord Cornwallis finds himself obliged to call on the general officers, and the commanding officers of regiments in particular, and in general on the officers of the army, to assist him in putting a stop to the licentious conduct of the troops, and in saving the wretched inhabitants from being robbed, and in the most shocking manner ill-treated by those to whom they had a right to look for safety and protection."[2] On Sept. 10, 1798, Mr Wickham writes from London to Lord Castlereagh in a "private and confidential letter":—"I am desired by the Duke of Portland, as well as by Mr Pelham, to send your lordship, confidentially, the enclosed extract of a letter written from Waterford by an officer of the Guards of acknowledged merit, and to mention to your lordship that letters to the same effect generally, written

---

[1] July 24, 1799. "Cornwallis Correspondence," ii. p. 369.
[2] "Cornwallis Correspondence," ii. p. 395.

in still stronger terms, are daily received from officers of that part of the corps which is now in Ireland."[1] "I dread," says the writer of the extract referred to, "the indiscipline of the Irish militia; friends and foes are all the same to them, and they will plunder indiscriminately advancing or retreating, and, from what I have heard, no effort is made to restrain them. The dread the inhabitants have of the presence of a regiment of militia is not to be told; they shut up their shops, hide whatever they have, and, in short, all confidence is lost wherever they make their appearance."[2] In a letter directly addressed to Mr Pitt, Lord Cornwallis described the militia as a force "on which no dependence whatever can be placed, and which Abercromby too justly described by saying that they were only formidable to their friends."[3]

---

[1] "Castlereagh Correspondence," i. p. 341.

[2] This extract is dated August 29, 1798. It begins with an allusion to the Killala expedition. "Castlereagh Correspondence," i. p. 342.

[3] September 25, 1798. "Cornwallis Correspondence," ii., p. 413. In General Orders, dated February 26, 1798, Sir R. Abercromby thus expressed himself:—"The very disgraceful frequency of Courts-Martial, and the many complaints of the conduct of the troops in this kingdom, having too unfortunately proved the army to be in a state of licentiousness, which must render it formidable to every one but the enemy, the Commander-in-Chief thinks," &c. Sir R. Abercromby's action placed the Cabinet in difficulty. "An extraordinary sensation has been created," Portland wrote on the 11th of March 1798 to Lord Camden, who was then Lord-Lieutenant, "by Sir Ralph Abercromby's general order. Can it be genuine? And if genuine, for what purpose was it issued, and how was it allowed? Our friends here (in England) cannot repress their regret at the triumph which they conceive Lord Moira and his adherents, and indeed all the disaffected, will claim over the Chancellor and the heads of your government. The Irish, whom I have seen, and whose conversation has been reported to me, conceive that there must be some division in the government; that you must have been deluded or intimidated; that protection is to be withdrawn from them; that they will be sacrificed or forced to join the insurgents. I assure your Excellency, I must request a full and immediate explanation, which will enable me to give that

A letter written by Captain Taylor, by the direction of Lord Cornwallis, to Lieutenant-General Craig, throws some light on the conduct of the military:—

"Having laid before the Lord-Lieutenant the proceedings of a General Court-Martial, held by your orders, in Dublin Barracks on Saturday the 13th instant, of which Colonel the Earl of Enniskillen was president, I am directed to acquaint you that his Excellency entirely disapproves of the sentence of the above Court-Martial, acquitting Hugh Whollaghan of a cruel and deliberate murder, of which, by the clearest evidence, he appears to have been guilty. Lord Cornwallis orders the Court-Martial to be immediately dissolved, and directs that Hugh Whollaghan shall be dismissed from the corps of yeomanry in which he served, and that he shall not be received into any other corps of yeomanry in this kingdom. His Excellency further desires that the above may be read to the president and members of the Court-Martial in open court." In a postscript, Captain Taylor adds:—"I am also directed to desire that a new Court-Martial may be immediately convened for the trial of such prisoners as may be brought before them, and that none of the officers who sat upon Hugh Whollaghan be admitted as members."[1] The editor of the "Cornwallis Correspondence" says the facts connected with this case were shortly these:— "A party of the Mount Kennedy Corps of yeomanry, one of whom was Whollaghan, were patrolling at night. They entered a cabin occupied by a woman named Dogherty and her son, who was at that time eating his

satisfaction to our friends and to the public in general which has hitherto uniformly attended every measure of your Excellency's administration."
—Froude's "English in Ireland," iii. pp. 353, 354.

[1] October 18, 1798. "Cornwallis Correspondence," ii. pp. 419, 420.

supper. Whollaghan charged him with having been a rebel, and declared he would kill him. The young man begged the soldier to spare his life, and expressed his readiness to go before a magistrate. Whollaghan, however, twice snapped his piece at him, and one of his comrades coming in fired and broke Dogherty's arm, although the poor mother, seeing their murderous intentions, endeavoured to seize the muzzle of his gun. Whollaghan, in spite of her prayers and entreaties, deliberately levelled at Dogherty, who was lying on the floor, and shot him dead. A permanent Court-Martial, consisting of Lord Enniskillen, president, a Major and three Captains of the 5th Dragoons, one officer of the Fermanagh Militia, and one of the 68th, was sitting at Dublin, and Whollaghan was brought before them. The facts above stated were not denied, but the defence was that Dogherty had been a rebel, though now provided with a protection, and that Whollaghan was a very loyal subject. To prove this some evidence was tendered, and, as it was mostly hearsay, was very improperly admitted. The sentence pronounced on the prisoner was that 'this Court do find that he did shoot and kill Thomas Dogherty, a rebel, but do acquit him of any malicious or wilful intention of murder.'"[1]

Lord Cornwallis' severe censure of the conduct of the court martial naturally arrested attention in England. Lord Camden had been his immediate predecessor in the office of Viceroy. It was during his administration that Lord Carhampton and Sir Ralph Abercromby had felt themselves constrained to resign the post of Commander of the Forces in Ireland. It was during his administration likewise that Lord Moira, in a speech which I have quoted, described the reign of terror, of

[1] "Cornwallis Correspondence," ii. p. 420.

which he had been an eye-witness. Lord Camden (whose sister was the second wife of Lord Londonderry, Lord Castlereagh's father) appointed Lord Castlereagh Keeper of the Privy Seal in Ireland. On the sudden departure of Mr Pelham, Lord Castlereagh was appointed to undertake the duty of Chief Secretary to His Excellency, as the *locum tenens* of Mr Pelham, who, it may be remembered, went to England when the "system of horrors" began. Lord Castlereagh continued so to act when Lord Camden was succeeded in office by Lord Cornwallis. Lord Camden was much annoyed at Lord Cornwallis' action in the matter of the Whollaghan Court Martial, and in a letter to Lord Castlereagh, marked "secret," he did not conceal his feelings. Lord Camden had at one time some fault to find with Lord Castlereagh.[1] Writing to him on the 4th of February 1793, he says, "I really hope you will not suffer your national feeling to carry you too far," etc.[2] From the tone of Lord Camden's letter, we may, I think, conclude that Lord Castlereagh had taken the sapient counsel. "Secret, Nov. 4, 1798. Dear Castlereagh,—Letters from Pelham and from Elliot will have informed you of Pelham's having declined to return to Ireland. I did not, therefore, think it necessary to write to you upon the subject. I understand Lord Cornwallis feels as he ought to do towards you. Mr Pitt is disposed as much as possible to your appointment, and although I believe there are others who entertain strong prejudices against the appointment of

---

[1] "Castlereagh Correspondence,", i. p. 159. Lord Camden was then Lord Bayham. This letter, embodying the views of Lord Fitzwilliam's succession in the Vice-Royalty, is worthy of perusal.

[2] When Lord Castlereagh entered the Irish Parliament in 1790 Mr Froude describes him as "then an ardent patriot." "English in Ireland," iii. p. 11.

an Irishman to be Secretary to the Lord Lieutenant, yet your merits will, I doubt not, overcome these objections." "By a short letter I wrote to you you may have perceived the opinion I entertain of the letter written by Captain Taylor to General Craig. I think the ends of justice would have been completely answered by a disapprobation of the sentence was the case perfectly clear; and the warmest advocate for discipline must have been satisfied with the farther step of dissolving the court martial, but to add that no member who sat on that court martial should be chosen for the future ones is very severe. I have from the first moment of reading the sentence felt upon it as I now do, and my sentiments are by no means changed." Lord Camden then alludes to his own Viceroyalty:—" How long is it, my dear Lord C., since *we* ordered an exclusive armament of supplementary yeomen in the North and of Mr Beresford's corps in Dublin? How many months have elapsed since we could *not decidedly* trust any bodies of men but those who are now so highly disapproved of? That the violence of some of the partisans of the Protestant interest should be repressed I believe you know I sincerely think, but that a condemnation of them should take place will infinitely hurt the English interest in Ireland. All these circumstances make me feel less rejoiced than I should otherwise do at an event which you so much deserve;[1] and I am truly sorry that my feelings and reflections both urge me to write as I have done upon this subject. I hardly know how to write it under your circumstances, but I rather conjecture from your silence that your opinion on this letter is not widely different. The great question of Union will be hurt by this measure, as, however *unjustly*, it will indispose, I

[1] Lord Castlereagh's appointment as Chief Secretary.

fear, a very important party to whatever seems to be a favourite measure of government."[1]

Of course the mildness of Lord Cornwallis' government was a subject of animadversion by the advocates of stern measures in England. The Viceroy thus defends himself to the Duke of Portland :—" Your Grace may be assured that I shall omit no means in my power to encourage and animate the whole body of yeomanry to a faithful and active discharge of their duty; but I can never permit them to take advantage of their military situation to pursue their private quarrels and gratify their personal resentments, or to rob or murder at their discretion any of their fellow-subjects whom they may think proper on their own authority to brand with the name of rebels."[2] To General Ross Lord Cornwallis repels the charge of leniency which had been advanced against him :—" You write," he says, " as if you really believed that there was any foundation for all the lies and nonsensical clamour about my lenity. On my arrival in this country I put a stop to the burning of houses and murder of the inhabitants by the yeomen, or any other persons who delighted in that amusement, to the flogging for the purpose of extorting confession, and to the free quarters which comprehended universal rape and robbery throughout the whole country."[3]

The picture drawn by Lord Cornwallis is dark, but the reality was still darker. " The evidence of Lord Cornwallis," says Mr Goldwin Smith, " is of course the best ; but the charges of cruelty and brutality which are authenticated by his correspondence are far from being

---

[1] " Castlereagh Correspondence," i. pp. 424-426.
[2] March 11, 1799. " Secret and Confidential.". " Cornwallis Correspondence," iii. p. 74.
[3] April 15, 1799. " Cornwallis Correspondence," iii. p. 89.

the worst that have been brought. Besides indiscriminate butchery and the more than savage use of torture, they are very circumstantially accused of having committed the grossest outrages and barbarities on women, and even of having massacred children. They are accused of having condemned to death by court-martial a boy of fifteen, and of having brought him to be executed at his mother's door." " The murders and other atrocities committed by the Jacobins were more numerous than those committed by the Orangemen, and as the victims were of higher rank they excited more indignation and pity; but in the use of torture the Orangemen seem to have reached a pitch of fiendish cruelty which was scarcely attained by the Jacobins." [1]

" I say," said Mr Grey in the English House of Commons, " I was sorry to hear the right hon. gentleman (Mr Pitt) justify the acts of severity which have been used in that country (Ireland). I say that nothing can render torture necessary in the present state of civilization in Europe. Will the right hon. gentleman, or will any man justify the practice of torture for the purpose of gaining political information. Nor has anything which the right hon. gentleman said about connection with the enemy justified a practice so abhorrent to humanity." [2] " My Lords," said the Duke of Bedford in the English House of Lords, " were I to enter into a detail of the horrible acts which have been done in Ireland, the picture would appal the stoutest heart. It could be proved that the most shocking atrocities have been perpetrated; but, indeed, what could be expected, if men kept in strict discipline were all at once allowed to give loose to their fury and their passions?" " It is known that

---

[1] " Irish History and Irish Character," p. 174, 175.
[2] February 7, 1799. " Parliamentary Debates," vii. p. 701.

regiments have published declarations in which they state that certain persons shall find, before they are delivered unto the civil power, that such and such a regiment is not to be trifled with."[1] Lord Moira, speaking in the English House of Lords on March 19, 1799, referred to "the modes of indiscriminate and savage torture which had been adopted without compunction, and persevered in without remorse. The picketings, the burning of houses, the rapes, and the numberless other outrages that had been perpetrated with the view, as it was whimsically said, of crushing disaffection, were surely the most extravagant means that any Government ever employed for extinguishing the discontents of a nation."[2]

On the 23d March 1801, Lord Clare, the Lord Chancellor of Ireland, actually defended in the English House of Lords the practice of torture. We read that he "adverted to the report that he was an advocate of torture. The foundation for that report," he said, "he recollected well, and should state it to the House. A blacksmith had been apprehended who, there was great reason to believe, had been engaged in framing pike heads. After various means being tried in vain to force him to confess where he had concealed them, he was placed upon the picket. There he had not remained half a minute when he told where five hundred might be found, and there they were found accordingly."[3] Lord Moira, in reply to the noble lord, said :—" That was not the only instance in which torture had been applied to extort confessions of guilt. In a vast variety of other cases it had been resorted to to compel persons to

---

[1] March 22, 1798. "Parliamentary Debates," vii. p. 755.
[2] "Parliamentary Register," viii. p. 301.
[3] Woodfall's "Parliamentary Debates," i. p. 544.

criminate their neighbours, and in these cases the application of the torture was not for half a minute only, but for whole hours, and that at repeated times. On confessions so obtained it was impossible to form an accurate and wholesome judgment."[1] This was not the first occasion on which Lord Clare defended the use of torture, nor was the instance of the blacksmith the only case of torture within his knowledge. In February 1798, in the Irish House of Lords, we find him stating that the burning of houses by the military "could not be strictly justified, but that some examples were necessary to be made. As to the half-hanging a man of the name of Shaw, he denied that anything more was done than tying the rope around his neck to induce him to confess."[2] Lord Moira was not mistaken when he said that, although "he could not altogether rely on his memory with regard to what had passed in the debate on this subject in the Irish Parliament, he might venture to assert that the case of the blacksmith was not then stated by the noble and learned lord in the same manner as it was this night."[3]

Under this "system of horrors" the cause of the Union prospered. So early as the 25th September 1798 Lord Cornwallis writes to Mr Pitt:—"The principal people here are so frightened that they would, I believe, readily consent to a Union, but then it must be a Protestant Union; and even the Chancellor (Lord Clare), who is the most right headed politician in the country, will not hear of the Roman Catholics sitting in the United Parliament."[4]

[1] Woodfall's "Parliamentary Debates," i. p. 544.
[2] "Grattan's Life," iv. p. 330.
[3] Woodfall's "Parliamentary Debates," i. p. 544.
[4] "Cornwallis Correspondence," ii. p. 414.

CHAPTER VII.

THE UNION AND EXCEPTIONAL LEGISLATION AND MARTIAL LAW.

I HAVE endeavoured to sketch the effect produced on the country by the numbers and the conduct of the military during the period the measure of the Union was under discussion. To complete the picture it must be borne in mind that the country was likewise under martial law, that the Habeas Corpus Act was suspended, and that exceptional legislation in the form of Insurrection Acts, Indemnity Acts, and Rebellion Acts, was fully developed. Thus, on the 24th July 1798, Lord Cornwallis writes to Major-General Ross, who had served with him in the War of the American Independence:—
"Except in the instance of the six state trials that are going on here, there is no law either in town or country but martial law, and you know enough of that to see all the horrors of it even in the best administration of it, judge then how it must be conducted by Irishmen heated with passion and revenge."[1]

In a "private" letter from Lord Cornwallis to Lord

---

[1] "Cornwallis Correspondence," ii. p. 369. The trials referred to were those of the brothers Sheares, Byrne, Macan, Bond and Neilson, the leaders of the United Irishmen. They were "defended," like the vast majority of the political prisoners of the time, by Mr MacNally. The publication of the "Cornwallis Correspondence" in 1859 revealed the shameful fact that this person was a traitor in the pay of the Government. See "Cornwallis Correspondence," iii. p. 320.

Castlereagh, dated September 26, 1799, we have a vivid picture of the state of the country. "There is certainly mischief working in various parts of the country, and, Marsden thinks, in Dublin and its vicinity. In the meantime the same wretched business of courts-martial, hanging, transporting, &c., attended by all the dismal scenes of wives, sisters, fathers kneeling and crying, is going on as usual, and holds out a comfortable prospect for a man of any feeling."[1] Lord Cornwallis did not, however, use sufficient vigour to satisfy his friends. "I am strongly pressed," he writes, "to use the same coercive measures which so totally failed last year, but I cannot be brought to think that flogging and free quarter will ever prove good opiates."[2] Again, "The greatest difficulty which I experience is to control the violence of our loyal friends, who would, if I did not keep the strictest hand upon them, convert the system of martial law (which God knows is of itself bad enough) into a more violent and intolerable tyranny than that of Robespierre. The vilest informers are hunted out from the prisons to attack by the most barefaced perjury the lives of all who are suspected of being or of having been disaffected, and, indeed, every Roman Catholic of influence is in great danger. You will have seen by the addresses both in the north and south that my attempt to moderate that violence and cruelty which has once driven, and which, if tolerated, must again soon drive this wretched country into rebellion, is not reprobated by the voice of the country, although it has appeared so culpable in the eyes of the absentees."[3]

[1] "Castlereagh Correspondence," ii. p. 406.
[2] Cornwallis to Viscount Brome, Dec. 26, 1798. "Cornwallis Correspondence," iii., p. 24. This nobleman was Lord Cornwallis' son-in-law.
[3] Cornwallis to Ross, Nov. 16, 1799. "Cornwallis Correspondence," iii. p. 145.

As we read these passages we cannot but be struck with admiration at the efforts of this kindly hearted nobleman to assuage the storm of vindictive passion that raged around him. Lord Camden wrote as we have seen to Lord Castlereagh, counting on his sympathy in condemning Lord Cornwallis for censuring the members of the Court-Martial, who acquitted Hugh Whollaghan of a charge of cruel and deliberate murder of which he had been proved guilty by the clearest evidence. The following incident will, I think, prove that Lord Camden had not mistaken his man. In a letter to Mr Wickham, Lord Castlereagh contrasts the advantages of a Bill authorising trial by court-martial with those of an Indemnity Act. The latter is defective, since "the responsibility of doing an act which in the eye of the law is, in strictness, murder, is too weighty to be encountered in the prospect of future indemnity."[1] Murder must be pardoned by anticipation before its commission. We find accordingly in the Castlereagh and Cornwallis Correspondence, some accounts of the exceptional legislation which had for its object the exemption of would-be murderers from a responsibility "too weighty to be encountered in the prospect of future indemnity."

On the meeting of Parliament in January 1799, a Statute was passed to indemnify all persons who had resorted to illegal measures. One of its provisions enacted that a jury should not convict if magistrates could prove that in what they had done they had acted for the purpose of suppressing the rebellion. This legislation, however, did not prevail to shield the malefactors. Lord Castlereagh, therefore, recom-

[1] 16th Nov. 1798. "Castlereagh Correspondence," i. p. 447. See Appendix A.

mends a remedy which he thus explains in a "private" letter, dated April 26, 1799, to the Duke of Portland. "At the late assizes in Clonmel, two actions were tried and verdicts obtained upon them against Mr Fitzgerald, for acts done by him during the rebellion in the execution of his office as High Sheriff. In consequence of this various actions have been brought not only against him but against many other magistrates who were active in repressing the disaffected. Nothing could be more fatal to the King's interests than an impression obtaining that the Bill of Indemnity was inadequate to protect those who had acted for the public service with good intentions, however, in a moment of struggle and warmth they might have erred in point of discretion. Nothing can be more explicit than the words of the law are upon this subject; and there can be no doubt that if soundly and clearly expounded by the Bench, and correctly acted upon by the jury, protection is completely afforded by them to every man whom the Legislature could possibly mean to protect. But when these transactions come to be reviewed at a cooler moment the act of violence is proved, when it is impossible for the defendant to adduce evidence to the whole of the circumstances under which he acted. There is a laudable disposition in the Bench to condemn what appears, as the case is stated, a severity not altogether called for; the circumstances are strongly coloured by the plaintiff's counsel, and the jury ultimately find their verdict rather upon the question of whether the defendant exercised a sound discretion than whether he acted *bona fide* with a fair intention for the public service. Foreseeing that many actions tending to keep alive animosities are likely to be brought to trial, it has been thought expedient by the Crown lawyers, with the approbation of the Chancellor (Lord Clare), to introduce a short Bill requiring the jury in all actions when the defendant pleads that he acted for the suppression of the Rebellion, in case they find for the plaintiff, to find that the defendant acted maliciously, and not with an intent to suppress the Rebellion, otherwise the verdict to be null and void, and that on all such actions it shall be competent for the judge to certify against the verdict if it shall be for the plaintiff, and upon such certificate a non-suit shall be entered. It is considered that this will bring the jury to decide in all cases upon the true question at issue the *quo animo* with which the defendant acted, as it would be a little hard upon the defendant to be prepared for years after the fact to prove that his conduct was altogether prudent or justified by the strict necessity of the case. The certificate of the judge will guard against the improper findings of disaffected juries to which a country so disturbed and corrupted cannot but be liable."[1]

Again we learn from the editor of the "Castlereagh Correspondence" the connection of the Union with exceptional legislation. In the month of March 1800, he tells us, "while the all-important measure of Union was still under discussion, the Irish Government, through their Attorney and Solicitor-General, submitted to the Commons two Bills, the one enabling military officers to act as magistrates, the other authorising them to try by martial law any persons for 'rebellion, sedition, or any crimes connected therewith.'"[2] The practical effect of this legislation was to hand over the people of

[1] "Castlereagh Correspondence," ii. pp. 280-82.
[2] *Ibid.*, iii. p. 214.

Ireland, bound hand and foot, to merciless military power.

Notwithstanding what Lord Castlereagh terms "the laudable disposition of the Bench," I question whether the unfortunate victims of this system of horrors had much to choose between the military and civil power. Here is Lord Cloncurry's experience of the administration of justice in Ireland in 1797. "It happened that the barony of Carbery, in the county of Kildare, was proclaimed under the Insurrection Act, and a camp established in it, which was occupied by the Fraser Fencibles. One evening the commanding officer, a Captain Fraser, returning to camp from Maynooth, where he had dined and drank freely, passed through a district belonging to my father, which was very peaceable and had not been included in the proclamation. As Captain Fraser rode through the village of Cloncurry, attended by an orderly dragoon, just as the summer sun was setting, he saw an old man named Christopher Dixon upon the roadside engaged in mending his cart. The captain challenged him for being out after sunset, in contravention of the terms of the proclamation. Dixon replied that he was not in a proclaimed district, and that he was engaged in his lawful business, preparing his cart to take a load to Dublin the following day. The captain immediately made him prisoner, and placed him on horseback behind his orderly. The party proceeded about half a mile in this manner to a turnpike, where the officer got into a quarrel with the gatekeeper, and some delay took place, of which Dixon took advantage to beg of the turnpike man to explain that the district in which he was taken was not proclaimed, and that, therefore, there was no just ground for his arrest. While the altercation was proceeding the poor old man (he was almost eighty years of age) slipped off from the dragoon's horse and was proceeding homewards when the officer and soldier followed him, and having despatched him with sixteen dirk and sabre wounds, of which nine were declared to be mortal, they rode off to the camp. A coroner's inquest was held on the body, and a verdict of wilful murder returned; whereupon Mr Thomas Ryan, a magistrate, and the immediate landlord of Dixon under my father, proceeded to the camp with a warrant for the apprehension of Captain Fraser, who, however, was protected by his men, and Mr Ryan was driven off. Mr Ryan applied to my father, who sent me with him to Lord Carhampton, then commander-in-chief in Ireland. We were accompanied by Colonel (after General Sir George) Cockburn, and Mr Ryan, having produced the warrant, and Colonel Cockburn, having pointed out the provision in the Mutiny Act, bearing upon the case, we formally demanded the body of Fraser, which his Lordship refused to surrender. At the next assizes, Captain Fraser marched into Athy with a band playing before him and gave himself up for trial. The facts were clearly proved, but the sitting judge, Mr Toler (afterwards Lord Norbury), instructed the jury that 'Fraser was a gallant officer, who had only made a mistake,' 'that if Dixon was as good a man as he was represented to be it was well for him to be out of this wicked world, but if he was as bad as many others in the neighbourhood (looking at me who sat beside him on the bench), it was well for the country to be quit of him.' The captain and his orderly were acquitted accordingly."

"Such," says Lord Cloncurry, "was the training of both peasant and soldier for the bloody civil war of the ensuing year."[1]

[1] Personal Recollections of Valentine, Lord Cloncurry, pp. 49-51. "Mr Toler (Lord Cloncurry adds in a note) was at the time, as well as my memory serves me, Solicitor-General, but sitting as Judge of Assize." The Irish Judges had become independent in 1782, and could not, therefore, be relied on by the Government. The Executive Government thought proper to permit one of their own law officers, a Member of Parliament, associated in the framing of Coercion Acts, to sit on the Judicial Bench to carry out the policy of his masters and to shield the murderers. Mr Toler became Solicitor General in 1789. He was not elevated to the Bench till 1800. He was even more zealous in procuring convictions when convictions were required by the Government. He occupies in Ireland the position assigned in England to Jeffreys and to Scroggs. The agony of his fellow-creatures was his delight; he seemed to take a fiendish pleasure in pronouncing sentence of death. Mr Froude admits the Government were in possession of the secrets of the leaders of the Rebellion in 1798 long before its explosion. With such machinery at the disposal of Government, Mr Froude's contention that those men were not arrested from want of available evidence is incredible. See "English in Ireland," iii. pp. 327-328.

CHAPTER VIII.

THE CIRCUMSTANCES ATTENDING THE FIRST INTRODUCTION OF THE UNION TO THE IRISH PARLIAMENT.

MR SHERIDAN stated very succinctly the means by which the Union was carried, when he declared, from his place in the English Parliament, that Mr Pitt, in his promotion of that measure, had two allies, intimidation and corruption.[1] I have hitherto confined myself to tracing in very faint outline the methods of intimidation. We must now consider the influence of the twin sister of intimidation—corruption. We will find in every stage of this transaction, intimidation and corruption walking hand in hand. It will I think be more convenient to deal separately with the process of corruption before the 22nd January 1799, when the measure of the Union was first proposed in the Irish Parliament, reserving for a separate notice the dealings of Lord Castlereagh with the Irish Constitution, between the 22nd January 1799 and the 1st August 1800, when the Act of Legislative Union received the Royal Assent. In a " private and confidential letter," dated 16th November 1798, Lord Camden thus counsels Lord Castlereagh on the question of the Union, which he apprehends had been mismanaged by Lord Cornwallis, "I conclude

[1] February 7, 1799. "Parliamentary Debates," vii. p. 683.

you have only one line to follow, viz., to talk a firm and decided language, to find out by as much address as possible the expectations of individuals and the objections of bodies of men, and to lose no time in securing the one and counteracting the others."[1]

Four days afterwards Lord Cornwallis writes to the Duke of Portland :—" Lord Castlereagh's appointment gave me great satisfaction ; and although I admit the propriety of the general rule, yet he is so unlike an Irishman, I think he has a just claim to an exception in his favour." " When I, therefore, found a man in the actual execution of the duty possessed of all the necessary qualifications,[2] with a perfect knowledge of the characters and connections of the principal personages in this country, I felt it to be my duty at this very important moment to press his appointment in the very strongest terms."[3] The reasons which justified Lord Castlereagh's appointment are most candidly stated. He was clearly to influence the principal personages, with whose circumstances he was intimately acquainted. We find that Mr Pitt himself was engaged in a similar attempt to influence the Speaker of the Irish Parliament, Mr

[1] "That it would have been wiser to have received the voice and the conversation and the influence of some leading characters before this authority (to speak confidentially, etc.) had been given, I have little doubt, but since Lord Cornwallis is so far authorised, and I doubt not has committed himself, I conclude," etc. "Castlereagh Correspondence," i. pp. 448-449.

[2] To Lord Camden belongs the discredit of having placed Lord Castlereagh in the execution of this duty, on personal and family considerations.

[3] "Private," Nov. 20, 1798. "Cornwallis Correspondence," ii. p. 439. Lord Cornwallis says in the same letter that several excellent persons were named for the post, "but scarcely a hope was entertained that any one of them would accept the office." It does not, however, appear that any of these gentlemen were given the opportunity of declining the appointment.

Foster, who was, however, proof against temptation. Mr Pitt, writing to Lord Cornwallis, gives an account of his conversation with the Speaker on the question of the Union, to which he hopes that statesman will give a fair support if made "palatable to him personally." "It would," Mr Pitt remarks, "as it seems to me, be well worth while, for this purpose, to hold out to him the prospect of an English peerage, with, if possible, some ostensible situation and a provision for life, to which he would naturally be entitled on quitting the chair." In this letter there are the following plain directions to bribe the rank and file of the House of Commons:— "In the interval previous to your Session there will, I trust, be full opportunity for communication and arrangement with individuals on whom I am inclined to believe the success of the measure will wholly depend."[1]

This corruption was not, however, to be confined to the members of the House. It was likewise to be exercised out of doors. Thus Lord Castlereagh is able to inform Mr Wickham "the principal provincial papers have been secured, and every attention will be paid to the press generally."[2] "Your Grace," writes Lord Cornwallis to the Duke of Portland, "will probably have seen in the papers an account of the violence which disgraced the meeting of the barristers, and of the miserable figure which the friends of the Union made

---

[1] "Private," Nov. 17, 1798. "Cornwallis Correspondence," ii. p. 440. "I maintain," says the Duke of Argyll, denying altogether the immorality of the Union, and taking exception to the whole argument, "that the conduct of Mr Pitt was pure and elevated conduct, with a pure and elevated purpose." Lord Brabourne commends to his readers the "brave words" of the duke. "Facts and Fictions in Irish History," p. 35.

[2] "Secret," Nov. 23, 1798. "Cornwallis Correspondence," ii. p. 444.

on the division of 32 against 162."[1] The editor of the
"Cornwallis Correspondence" informs us in a foot-note
that "the Union was violently opposed by almost all the
barristers except such as then held office under the
Crown, or were in expectation of preferment. Of the
thirty-two that composed the minority at this meeting,
all but five had before the close of 1803 obtained their
reward. Amongst them were numbered five judges,
sixteen County Court judges, two Officers in Chancery,
three Commissioners of Bankrupts, and one Commis-
missioner of the Board of Compensation." The Duke of
Portland instructs Lord Cornwallis, *inter alia*, "that the
conduct of individuals upon this subject will be considered as the test of their disposition to support the
King's Government."[2] This intimation seems to be
clear enough, but three days later the Duke of Portland
is anxious to make his meaning plainer. Writing again
to Lord Cornwallis, he says:—" I desire to assure your
Excellency in the most explicit and unqualified terms,
that every one of the King's servants, as well as myself,
will consider themselves indissolubly obliged to use
their best endeavours to fulfil whatever engagements
your Excellency may find it necessary or deem it
expedient to enter into with a view of accomplishing
the Union of Great Britain and Ireland."[3]

The following extracts from the letters of the persons
to whom the management of the Union was intrusted
will need no comment. They were written on the eve
of the first introduction of the measure to Parliament on
January 22, 1799. Thus Lord Castlereagh writes to

[1] "Secret and Confidential," Dec. 15, 1798. "Cornwallis Correspondence," iii. p. 18.
[2] Dec. 21, 1798. "Cornwallis Correspondence," iii. p. 20.
[3] Dec. 24, 1798. "Castlereagh Correspondence," ii. p. 60.

First Introduction of the Union.

Mr Wickham on January 2, 1799:—"Most secret." "Already we feel the want, and indeed the absolute necessity of the *primum mobile*.[1] We cannot give that activity to the press which is requisite. We have good materials amongst the young barristers, but we cannot expect them to waste their time, and to starve into the bargain. I know the difficulties, and shall respect them as much as possible in the extent of our expenditure, but, notwithstanding every difficulty, I cannot help most earnestly requesting to receive £5000 in bank notes by the first messenger."[2] Then we have Mr Wickham's reply to this communication, which I give in full.

"Private and most secret.

"WHITEHALL, *Jan.* 7, 1799. 20 *m. past* 5.

"MY DEAR LORD,—Immediately upon the receipt of your Lordship's letter of the 2d instant, marked Most Secret, I waited on the Duke of Portland at Burlington House, who, without loss of time, wrote both to Mr Pitt and Lord Grenville on that part of the letter which seemed to press the most, and I have the satisfaction to be able to inform your Lordship that a messenger will be sent off from hence in the course of to-morrow with

---

[1] In a letter in the *Dublin Evening Mail* of the 22nd September 1886, the Rev. Professor Galbraith, S.F.T.C.D., thus comments on this expression: "The *primum mobile* was a term of the Ptolemaic Astronomy expressing the outermost of the revolving spheres of the Universe which was supposed to give motion to all the others. As the *primum mobile* was necessary to put in motion the machinery of the Universe, so the money Lord Castlereagh required was indispensable for putting into motion the machinery which carried the Union.

[2] "Cornwallis Correspondence," iii. p. 27. This letter is not to be found in the "Castlereagh Correspondence," although two other letters of the same date are inserted.

the remittance particularly required for the present moment, and that the Duke of Portland has every reason to hope that means will soon be found of placing a larger sum at the Lord-Lieutenant's disposal. Believe me, &c. "WILLIAM WICKHAM."[1]

The editor of the "Cornwallis Correspondence" states that the numbers of the notes amounting to £5000 are still preserved in the State Paper Office. Lord Castlereagh thus replies to Mr Wickham:—

"Private.
"DUBLIN CASTLE, *Jan.* 10, 1799.

"MY DEAR SIR,—I have only a moment to acknowledge the receipt of your letters of the 7th. The *contents* of the messenger's despatches are very interesting. Arrangements with a view to further communications of the same nature will be highly advantageous, and the Duke of Portland may depend on their being carefully applied,—I am, &c. "CASTLEREAGH."[2]

This work was not so congenial to Lord Cornwallis. However blunted his moral sensibilities may have been, he was not wholly deaf to the promptings of conscience, nor entirely bereft of the feelings of a gentleman. He thus writes to General Ross on Jan. 21, 1799:—" Here I am embarked in all my troubles, and employed in a business which is ill-suited to my taste, and for which I am afraid I am not qualified. We think ourselves tolerably strong as to numbers, but so little confidence is to be placed in professions, and people change their

[1] "Castlereagh Correspondence," ii. p. 82. "Cornwallis Correspondence," iii. p. 34. I have quoted the letter as it appears in the "Cornwallis Correspondence." The letter is somewhat fuller in the "Castlereagh Correspondence."

[2] "Cornwallis Correspondence," iii. p. 34.

opinions here with so little ceremony, that no man who knows them can feel his mind quite at ease on that subject. The demands of our friends rise in proportion to the appearance of strength on the other side; and you who know how I detest a job, will be sensible of the difficulties which I must often have to keep my temper, but still the object is great, and perhaps the salvation of the British Empire may depend upon it. I shall, therefore, as much as possible, overcome my detestation of the work in which I am engaged, and march on steadily to my point."[1]

The Union was first introduced to the notice of the public as a matter for discussion. Members of Parliament were invited to give their opinions on the subject, and to think it over in all its bearings. It was considered advisable to accustom the public mind to think of the measure as at least a debateable question. It was felt that a great step would be gained if such a matter could be discussed with temper. Ministers feared the distinct and decided refusal of the people to sacrifice their national existence, but felt that a nation that deliberates on the extinction of its dearest rights is lost. Lord Castlereagh, on 1st December 1798, thus writes to Sir G. F. Hill, the Member for Derry:—"The public sentiment at this critical moment cannot be in more discreet and judicious hands. As to argument on the question, the pamphlet which I enclose is a magazine of the first materials. Reprint it at Derry, and circulate it as widely as possible; discourage warmth or early declarations on either side; keep the public mind in a deliberate state, and I am sanguine enough to hope the event must be favourable."[2]

---

[1] "Cornwallis Correspondence," iii. pp. 39, 40.
[2] "Castlereagh Correspondence," ii. p. 33.

We have seen that an effort had been made to bribe Mr Foster, the Speaker of the Irish House of Commons, but without success. A similar attack had been made on the principles of Sir John Parnell, who succeeded Mr Foster in the office of Chancellor of the Exchequer, and whose position and talents would have rendered his conversion to the Unionist cause a matter of paramount importance. Lord Castlereagh, it seems, had interviewed Sir John Parnell in London, but the conversation had not been satisfactory to his Lordship. There was, however, a difficulty in the matter of dismissals, which is well explained by Lord Cornwallis :—" I have already felt it a question of considerable delicacy to decide in what instances and at what period it was expedient to remove persons from office who have either taken a decided line against the measure, or who, without acting publicly, hold a language equally prejudicial to its success, and equally inconsistent with their connection with Government. In the instance of Mr J. C. Beresford, whose conduct has been very hostile at many of the Dublin meetings, the difficulty has been peculiarly felt. With a view of impressing our friends with the idea of our being in earnest, his dismissal seemed desirable ; on the other hand, as we profess to encourage discussion, and neither to precipitate Parliament or the country on the decision, much less to force it against public sentiment, there seemed an objection to a very early exercise of ministerial authority on the inferior servants of the Crown." [1]

[1] Cornwallis to Portland, Jan. 11, 1799. " Secret " " Cornwallis Correspondence," iii. p. 35. The letter goes on to state that Lord Cornwallis thought " it expedient to proceed in the first instance with the Chancellor of the Exchequer " (Sir J. Parnell).

The dismissal of Sir John Parnell from one of the highest posts in the kingdom on the eve of the Union debate, would, it was thought, have a salutary effect. On his arrival from London, Lord Cornwallis had a conversation with him. Where, however, Lord Castlereagh failed, he could not hope to succeed. "On my finding, from a conversation I had with Sir John Parnell soon after he landed, that he was determined not to support the Union, I have notified to him his dismission from the office of Chancellor of the Exchequer, and I shall pursue the same line of conduct without favour or partiality whenever I may think it will tend to promote the success of the measure."[1]

The sentiments of Ministers on the Catholic question previous to the first debate in the Irish Parliament on the Union, may, I think, be gathered from the following correspondence. On the 16th October 1798, Lord Clare writes from London to Lord Castlereagh: "I have seen Mr Pitt, the Chancellor, and the Duke of Portland, who seem to feel very sensibly the critical situation of our damnable country, and that the Union alone can save it.[2] I should have

---

[1] Cornwallis to Portland, "Private and Confidential," Jan. 16, 1799. "Cornwallis Correspondence," iii. p. 38.

[2] Here are Lord Clare's public views respecting his "damnable country." "I hope I feel as becomes a true Irishman for the dignity and independence of my country. I would therefore elevate her to her proper station in the rank of civilised nations. I would advance her from the degraded post of a mercenary province to the proud station of an integral and governing member of the greatest empire in the world."—"English in Ireland," iii. p. 555. The passage is an extract from Lord Clare's speech in the Irish House of Lords on the 10th of February 1800, which, Mr Froude says, "was distinguished like all else which came from Clare, by keen unspareful truthfulness."—*Ibid.*, p. 551. I have directed attention to Lord Clare's speech in the Irish House of Commons in 1789, in reference to bribery, and to his defence of torture in both the Irish and English

hoped that what has passed would have opened the eyes of every man in England to the insanity of their past conduct with respect to the Papists of Ireland, but I can very plainly perceive that they were as full of their Popish projects as ever. I trust, and I hope I am not deceived, that they are fairly inclined to give them up, and to bring the measure forward unincumbered with the doctrine of emancipation. Lord Cornwallis has intimated his acquiescence on this point. Mr Pitt is decided upon it, and I think he will keep his colleagues steady." "If I have been in any manner instrumental in persuading the Ministers here to bring forward this very important measure, unencumbered with a proposition which must have swamped it, I shall rejoice very much in the pilgrimage which I have made."[1] "The claims of Catholics," Lord Cornwallis writes to the Duke of Portland, "will certainly be much weakened by their incorporation into the mass of British subjects, and the English Test Laws will form a strong barrier against their carrying the point for which they have so long contended."[2] Again, "The Catholics as a body still

House of Lords. Mr Froude considers this nobleman to have been ill-treated by England. "When Clare died, the best friend she ever had, she gave a sigh of relief at being rid of his oppressive presence. She permitted the scum of Dublin to dishonour his open grave, and has left his memory to be trampled on lest she should offend the prejudices of later generations of patriots by confessing the merits of the greatest statesman whom Ireland ever produced."—"English in Ireland," pp. 345-346. See Mr Lecky's observations on Lord Clare, "Leaders of Public Opinion," pp. 166, 167.

[1] "Castlereagh Correspondence," i. pp. 393, 394. Lord Clare was the first Irishman who held the post of Lord Chancellor of Ireland. He owed his preferment probably to the fact that he resembled Lord Castlereagh in being unlike an Irishman.

[2] "Secret," Dec. 24, 1798. "Cornwallis Correspondence," iii. p. 22. This is Lord Cornwallis' opinion after a conversation with Mr Bellew, a Catholic.

adhere to their reserve on the measure of Union."
" What line of conduct they will ultimately adopt when
decidedly convinced that the measure will be persevered
in on Protestant principles, I am incapable of judging.
I shall endeavour to give them the most favourable impressions, without holding out to them hopes of any
relaxation on the part of the Government, and shall
leave no effort untried to prevent an opposition to the
Union being made a measure of that party."[1]

[1] "I so much fear, should it be made a Catholic principle to resist the Union, that the favourable sentiments entertained by individuals would give way to party feeling, and deprive us of our principal strength in the South and West, which could not fail, at least for the present, to prove fatal to that measure."—"Secret and Confidential," Jan. 2, 1799. Cornwallis to Portland. "Cornwallis Correspondence," iii. pp. 28, 29.

CHAPTER IX.

THE DEFEAT OF THE UNION IN 1799.

I HAVE endeavoured in the preceding pages to show the manner in which the Irish Parliament and the Irish people were educated for the Union. The various means adopted by the British Government to bring Ireland into a proper frame of mind for the reception of that measure were thus admirably summarised by Mr (afterwards Lord) Plunket in the Irish House of Commons on the 22d January 1799. In order to apprehend clearly the force of the reference to France, it must be remembered that at the time this speech was delivered, the armies of the Revolution were supposed to entertain hopes of universal conquest. " I will be bold to say that licentious and impious France in all the unrestrained excesses to which anarchy and atheism have given birth, has not committed a more insidious act against her enemy than is now attempted by the professed champion of civilised Europe, against a friend and an ally in the hour of her calamity and distress—at a moment when our country is filled with British troops, when the loyal men of Ireland are fatigued with their exertions to put down rebellion— efforts in which they had succeeded before these troops arrived, whilst the Habeas Corpus Act is suspended, whilst trials by Court-Martial are carrying on in many parts of the kingdom, whilst the people are taught to think they have no right to meet or to deliberate, and whilst the great body of them are so palsied by their fears and worn down by their exertions that even this vital question is scarcely able to arouse them from their lethargy at a moment when we are distracted by domestic dissensions—dissensions artfully kept alive as the pretext for our present subjugation and the instrument of our future thraldom."[1] Mr Sheridan, speaking the day after in the English House of Commons, was scarcely less emphatic in his language than Mr Plunket. He likewise pointedly referred to France: "I hear much of French principles, but I wish gentlemen would not so closely follow French practices. Let us abstain from French corruption, French usurpation, French perfidy. Let us leave no ground for saying that we have made use of corruption to acquire ascendancy or subjugate the rights of any people. Let our Union be a Union of mind and spirit as well as of interest and power, not that sort of marriage in which fraud is the suitor and force the ratifier of the solemn contract."[2] Again, Mr Sheridan observes, "Ireland in her present temper must be beaten into this measure, and that Minister who shall make the bold experiment of flogging a whole nation into stupid beings, insensible alike to the duty she may owe to herself, insensible to rights of the present generation and the interests of the the race yet unborn, as much as to the arrogance and cupidity of those who shall inflict the blow or direct the torture, such a Minister," etc.[3] Mr (afterwards Lord) Grey thus expressed himself: "Look at the history of Ireland, and I say you will find that if it had not been

---

[1] "Plunket's Life," i. pp. 147, 148.
[2] January 23, 1799. "Parliamentary Debates," vii. 589.
[3] January 31, 1799. "Parliamentary Debates," vii. p. 662.

for the interference of British Councils and of British intrigue, none, or at least but few, of the evils which are now so much felt there would ever have taken place—evils of which the Government is the parent, yet which are now made the reason for taking away all the semblance of liberty among the Irish people. There are feuds, and religious animosities, and heats, and dissensions now in Ireland, and they distract that country. Who has excited them? Who has created these feuds and religious animosities? Who has created these dissensions? Who has endeavoured to set up one party in that country against another, and which has brought it into such a state of distraction? Government has caused all these evils, and Government is now making use of all these evils as a pretext for taking away the liberty of the people of Ireland. They have raised hopes, they have disappointed these hopes; they have excited alarms; they have created discontents, they have fostered animosities—all these things produce mischief, and that mischief is then given as the reason for taking away all the liberty of the people."[1] Still, despite all these insidious measures, when the Union was first proposed in the Irish Parliament it was virtually defeated. The story of that defeat I will tell in the words of Lord Cornwallis himself; writing the day after, he says—" In the House of Commons a similar address to that in the Lords was moved by Lord Tyrone, and seconded by Mr Fitzgerald, Member for the County of Cork, who both spoke firmly and shortly their sentiments in favour of an Union, but called upon the House merely to give the subject a discussion, without pledging them to the principle. Sir John Parnell followed, and opposed in a fair and candid manner, without

[1] February 7, 1799. "Parliamentary Debates," vii. p. 700.

entering into topics of violence, the principle and measure of an Union in general. He was followed by Mr George Ponsonby, who chiefly dwelt upon the incompetency of Parliament to entertain the subject, and made an animated appeal to the passions of the House to support the national pride and independence, and he concluded with an amendment, 'That the House would be ready to enter into any measure short of surrendering their free resident and independent legislature as established in 1782.' This produced a general debate, which lasted till one o'clock this day, when a division took place—in favour of the amendment, 105 : against, 106 ; and then a second division took place— for the Address, 107 ; against it, 105."[1] In another letter to the Duke of Portland, dated the same day, Lord Cornwallis says : " I have now only to express my sincere regret to your Grace that the prejudices prevailing amongst the Members of the Commons, countenanced and encouraged as they have been by the Speaker and Sir John Parnell, are infinitely too strong to afford me any prospect of bringing this measure with any chance of success into discussion in the course of the present session."[2] On the 24th January 1799 the Government sustained a defeat ; a motion of Sir Lawrence Parsons to expunge a paragraph from the Address being carried by 109 as against 104 who were in favour of its retention.[3] " The combined exertions," say Mr Lecky, " of almost all the men of talent, and of almost all the men of pure patriotism in the Parliament, were successful in 1799. The Government Bill was defeated by 109 to 104, and the illumination of Dublin attested the feeling of the

[1] January 23, 1749. Cornwallis to Portland. "Cornwallis Correspondence," iii. 41, 42.
[2] "Cornwallis Correspondence," iii. p. 45.   [3] *Ibid.*, iii. p. 49.

people. The national party did all that was in their power to secure their triumph, for they foresaw clearly that the struggle would be renewed. Ponsonby brought forward a resolution pledging the House to resist every future measure involving the principle it had condemned, but he was compelled eventually to withdraw it." [1]

Lord Cornwallis, as we have seen, acknowledged the defeat of the Government in the Irish Parliament on a subject of primary importance. In accordance with the practice of the Constitution as we understand it, the duty of a Ministry would be, under these circumstances, either to resign or to appeal by a dissolution from the decision of Parliament to the decision of the country. The Irish Administration adopted, however, neither of these courses, but proceeded with redoubled energy to corrupt and degrade the Parliament of Ireland, with a view to its eventual extinction. This episode affords a very striking illustration of the cardinal defect in the Irish Constitution. Ireland never had an Irish Cabinet responsible to the Irish Parliament, and through that Parliament to the Irish people. With such a Cabinet the Irish Parliament, unreformed though it was, and with a Roman Catholic population unemancipated, would still have preserved the liberties of its country. If Ireland, notwithstanding all those disadvantages, had possessed the blessing of a responsible Government, the Union could never have been carried.

[1] "Leaders of Public Opinion," p. 171.

CHAPTER X.

SOME OF THE MEANS BY WHICH THE UNION WAS CARRIED.

MR GRATTAN, speaking in the Irish House of Commons on the 26th May 1800 for the last time against the Union, thus described the series of measures of corruption pursued by the Government in the interval that elapsed from the first defeat of that measure in January 1796[1]:—"From the bad terms that attend the Union, I am naturally led to the foul means by which it has been obtained—dismissals from office, perversion of the Place Bill, sale of peerage, purchase of boroughs, appointment of sheriffs,—with a view to prevent the meeting of freemen and freeholders for the purpose of expressing their opinions on the subject of a legislative Union; in short, the most avowed corruption, threats, and stratagems, accompanied by martial law, to deprive a nation of her liberty." With a view to clearness, I will deal *seriatim* with some of the means adopted for the further political education of Ireland, and to render her more capable of appreciating the blessings to be showered on her by a legislative Union.

1. *Dismissals from Office.*

The Irish House of Commons consisted of 300 Members, 64 of whom were returned by the counties, 2

[1] "The measure," says Lord Londonderry, "when first submitted to the Parliament of Ireland, was roughly repulsed, and if it met with a better reception when laid a second time before that legislature, it is not going too far to affirm that to the tact, management, assiduity, and exertions of Lord Castlereagh its final success is mainly to be attributed."—"Castlereagh Correspondence," i. p. 14.

by the University, and 62 by cities and towns possessing an open franchise more or less popular in its form. No less than 172 Members were returned by close boroughs in which the nomination rested with a patron or the Crown. Only 128 out of the 300 owed their return to the semblance of popular choice.[1] Of these 300 Members 116 were placemen. The British House of Commons in 1800 consisted of 558 Members, and we have the authority of Mr Pitt for saying that at that time "the number of places held by Members did not exceed 52."[2]

In Ireland, therefore, out of 300 Members, 116 were placemen; whereas in England, out of 558 Members, only 52 were placemen.

On the eve of the first introduction of the measure to the Irish House of Commons, Sir John Parnell and Mr Fitzgerald, the Prime-Serjeant, were dismissed from offices which they had held with honour to themselves and their country, and which were the highest posts in the kingdom held at the pleasure of the Crown.[3] Their fate was of course a clear intimation of what the other place-holders had to expect in opposing the Government. "Did the right hon. gentleman (Mr Pitt) not know," Mr Sheridan asked in the British House of Commons, "that there were 116 placemen in the Irish House of Commons, and that, having made two great examples by dismissing the Chancellor of the Exchequer and the Prime-Serjeant, the others would be sure to remain stanch and true out of fear?"[4]

[1] "Irish Federalism," by Isaac Butt, p. 30.
[2] April 25, 1800. Woodfall's "Parliamentary Reports," ii. p. 494.
[3] "The Right Hon. James Fitzgerald, then Prime-Serjeant, was dismissed from office, having peremptorily refused to vote for the Union. The office of Prime-Serjeant, unknown in England, in Ireland took precedence of the Attorney and Solicitor-General."—Sir J. Barrington, p. 390.
[4] Feb. 7, 1799. "Parliamentary Debates," vii. p. 692.

Mr Sheridan thus explained away Mr Pitt's assertion that an equal proportion of the Irish House of Commons were in 1799 favourable to the measure of the Union:—" If he (Mr Pitt) would but look of what that division against it in the Commons was composed, he would discover that it contained almost all the country gentlemen; while, if he examined who composed that on the other side of the question, they would be almost all found to be under the influence of the Crown; if, besides this, the dismissals that had taken place in spite of the fair character of those who were removed—thus unjustly removed—from office, it was a shame to speak of anything like an equality between those who opposed and those who supported the Union." [1]

Some, however, of the placemen braved dismissal by voting against the Bill. On June 3, 1799, Lord Castlereagh writes a "private" letter to the Duke of Portland. "The Lord-Lieutenant received yesterday by the express your Grace's despatch of the 30th.[2] It is a great satisfaction to his Excellency to find that your Grace so perfectly coincides in opinion with him as to the measures which it becomes the King's Government to take at this moment towards those gentlemen holding offices who have failed in what they owed to the Crown on a late occasion. It is his Excellency's intention, before he dismisses them, to state to the principal friends of Government the grounds upon which the measure is taken, in order that they may be strongly impressed not only that this act of authority, which undoubtedly commits the Government with a very weighty and formidable party in the State, has his

[1] Jan. 31, 1799. "Parliamentary Debates," vii. p. 668.
[2] This despatch does not appear in the Castlereagh or Cornwallis "Correspondence."

Majesty's entire sanction and that of his Ministers, but that they have unequivocally the whole weight of the British Government at their back in the contest in which they are engaged." [1]

Mr Pitt seemed at first adverse to the dismissal of the placemen of less note. It was only in the progress of events that a wholesale dismissal was resolved on. Thus, in a " private" letter to Lord Cornwallis, written on the 26th January 1799, immediately on hearing of the division in the Irish House of Commons on the 23rd January, Mr Pitt says, "In this view it seems very desirable (if Government is strong enough to do it without too much immediate hazard) to mark by dismissal the sense entertained of the conduct of those persons in office who opposed. In particular, it strikes me as essential not to make an exception to this line in the instance of the Speaker's son. No Government can stand on a safe and respectable ground which does not show that it feels itself independent of him. With respect to persons of less note, or those who have been only neutral, more lenity may perhaps be advisable. On the precise extent of the line, however, your Lordship can alone judge on the spot; but I thought you would like to know from me directly the best view I can form of the subject." [2] The measure having been ostensibly submitted to the House for discussion, it seemed inconsistent to dismiss those who had given a candid opinion against it. It was only as the intentions of the Government became more apparent that the time came for Lord Castlereagh to announce unequivocally that the Irish ministry were engaged in a contest in which they had "the whole weight of the

---

[1] "Castlereagh Correspondence," ii. p. 327.
[2] "Cornwallis Correspondence," iii. p. 57.

British Government at their back." Mr (afterwards Lord) Grey was accurate in stating from his place in the English House of Commons,—"All holding offices under Government, even the most intimate friends of the Minister who have uniformly supported his administration till the present occasion, if they hesitated to vote as directed, were dismissed from office and stripped of all their employments."[1] A protest against the Union, signed by eighteen temporal and two spiritual Irish peers, of which the Duke of Leinster was the first signatory, states, among other reasons for objecting to the measure,—"The dismissal of the old steadfast friends of constitutional Government for their adherence to the constitution."[2]

2. *Abuse of the Place Bill.*

It requires but a slight acquaintance with the Constitutional History of Ireland before the Union to perceive that it consists of a prolonged struggle between the patriot party and the British Cabinet. The Irish patriots wished to gain for their country the constitutional privileges enjoyed by the English people. The British Cabinet deliberately obstructed, thwarted, and neutralised their efforts by bribery, force, or fraud. Thus an English Act of Anne provides that every Member of the House of Commons accepting an office under the Crown must vacate his seat, but may be re-elected, while persons holding offices created since the 25th October 1705 are incapacitated from being elected or re-elected Members of Parliament. The provisions of that Act were extended to Ireland

[1] Woodfall's "Parliamentary Reports," ii. p. 399.
[2] There is, in my opinion, no analogy between these dismissals and the ministerial resignations of modern times. The Government, on their defeat, declined either to dissolve or resign, but proceeded to procure a majority by the measures described in this chapter.

in 1793. The Irish Statute, however, only disqualified for seats in the Irish House of Commons the holders of all offices under the Crown or Lord-Lieutenant created after the date of its enactment. There were then 116 placemen in the Irish House of Commons. All the offices which they held were still tenable by Members of the House subject simply to the condition of re-election on their appointment. In 1789, only four years before the passing of this Act, 14 new places with increased salaries were granted to Members of the Irish House of Commons as an inducement to vote for the Government of England. No means were, however, provided till the passing of this Act for allowing a Member of Parliament in Ireland to vacate his seat by a manœuvre. Before 1793 a seat could be vacated by death, by being made a peer or a judge, or by taking holy orders, but by no other means whatever, save expulsion from the House. "A Bill," says Sir Jonah Barrington, "was brought in to vacate the seats of Members accepting offices under Government, omitting the term *bona fide* offices, thereby leaving the Minister a power of packing the Parliament. The Opposition, blinded by their honest zeal, considered this ruinous Bill a species of reform, and were astonished at the concession of a measure at once so popular, and which they conceived to be so destructive of ministerial corruption. The sagacity of Mr Pitt, however, clearly showed him that measure would put the Irish Parliament eventually into his hands, and the sequel proved that without that Bill worded as it was, the corruption by the Ministers, the Rebellion, force and terror combined, could not have effected the Union." Sir Jonah states that he positively refused his support to this Bill, "foreseeing its possible operation." The Ministers, he thinks, were "too subtle for Mr Grattan, and he heeded

not that fatal clause which made no distinction between real and nominal offices. He considerd not that though offices of real emolument could not be so frequently vacated and transferred as to give the Minister any very important advantage, those of nominal value might be daily given and resigned without observation, and that as the House was then constituted, the Minister might almost form the Commons at his pleasure."
"There are four nominal offices in Ireland—the Escheatorships of Leinster, Munster, Connaught, and Ulster; their emoluments are thirty shillings per annum. By means of these offices, Lord Castlereagh packed the Parliament in 1800. The Chiltern Hundreds in England are of the same nature, but the large number of the British Commons renders anything like packing Parliament for occasional purposes by that means impossible. Nor durst a British Minister practise that artifice except to a very limited extent."[1]

"A Place Bill," says Mr Lecky, "intended to guard the purity of Parliament against the corruption of Ministers, by compelling all who accepted offices to vacate their seats, had been recently passed, and the Ministers ingeniously availed themselves of this to consummate the triumph of corruption. According to the code of honour which then prevailed both in England and Ireland, the members of nomination boroughs who were unwilling to vote as their patrons directed, considered themselves bound to accept nominal offices, and thus vacate their seats, which were at once filled by stanch Unionists, in some instances by English and Scotch men wholly unconnected with Ireland."[2]

As early as the 16th May 1799, we find Lord Cornwallis refusing these nominal appointments to gentle-

---

[1] "Rise and Fall of the Irish Nation," pp. 339-341.
[2] "Leaders of Public Opinion," p. 180.

men, when those who were to succeed them in Parliament were opposed to the Union. "Lieutenant-Colonel Cole recently applied to Lord Castlereagh that he might be appointed Escheator of Munster, in order to vacate his seat upon his going abroad. It appeared in conversation that he intended to have his place supplied by Mr Balfour, who moved the resolutions against an Union at the county of Louth meeting, and suggested a recurrence to first principles if that measure should be carried. Mr Tighe had before applied for the same office for one of his members, with a view to sell the seat, on condition that the purchaser would not support an Union. These requests appeared to me of such a nature as to render it necessary to withhold my acquiescence from them."[1]

Lord Cornwallis, however, was able to utilise these nominal offices when the cause of the Union was likely thereby to be promoted. "When men," said Mr Plunket, in the Irish House of Commons, "would not be base enough openly to apostatise, their resignation was purchased, the Place Bill, which had been enacted to preserve the liberties of the subject, was converted into an instrument to oppress them, and no man suffered to vacate his seat unless he would stipulate an Unionist for his successor. The same Lord-Lieutenant who at first had declared his intention to submit the question to the uninfluenced sense of the country, frankly avowed his determination to abuse the prerogative for this scandalous purpose, and the noble Lord (Castlereagh), who had declared in full Parliament that he never would press the measure, even with a majority, against the free sense of Parliament, heard himself publicly branded with his shameful departure from that promise, in the

---

[1] "Cornwallis Correspondence," iii. p. 97. Colonel Cole was ordered to join his regiment serving abroad.

case of Colonel Cole, without having the hardihood to deny it. The British Minister thought this last act too indecent even for the meridian of Ireland, and the Parliament was the next day prorogued."[1]

On the 6th March 1800, Mr Ponsonby, who subsequently became Lord Chancellor of Ireland, and led the Whig party in the British House of Commons from 1808 till his death in 1817, entered into the details of the abuse of the Place Bill, speaking in the Irish House of Commons. " He was aware that a Place Bill had given a great accession of influence to the Government in this country. He did not mean to blame the Minister for availing himself of this influence in a fair way, provided he did not use it to procure a majority on any *particular* question which might be pending in Parliament. But within a few months, that is, since towards the close of the last sessions of Parliament till the present time, no less than sixty-three Members of that House had vacated their seats by accepting offices, principally nominal offices—as every man knew the Escheatorship of Munster was—that is, by the influence of this Act more than a full fifth of the whole representation of Ireland was changed. The people would observe that this change had been accompanied by another event— the Parliament which last session had marked this measure of Union with their pointed reprobation, and refused even to discuss it, had this session not only entered on the discussion, but had actually voted the principle."

The abuse of the Place Bill was not unperceived in England. It was severely stigmatised by the advocates of popular rights in both Houses of the British Parliament. Lord Holland, in the House of Lords, on 21st

[1] Jan. 22, 1800. " Plunket's Life," i. 185, 186.

April 1800, asked, "Whether it was doubted by any descriptions of persons in this kingdom that corruption and intimidation had not been practised to obtain a majority in support of the measure in both Houses of the Irish Parliament? Were ever such changes of Members in the gross seen but on a dissolution of Parliament as in the course of the last eight months?"[1] On the same day, Mr Grey, in the English House of Commons, echoed the statement of Mr Ponsonby in the Irish House. "A Bill framed for preserving the purity of Parliament was abused, and no less than sixty-three seats were vacated by their holders having received nominal offices."[2]

"The sense of Parliament," said Mr Grattan, on the 26th May 1800, "was against them; they change therefore the Parliament without recurring to the people, but procure a number of returns exceeding their present majority from private boroughs vacated with a view to return a court member who should succeed a gentleman that would not vote for the Union. Here there is a Parliament made by the Minister, not the people, and made for the question. Under these circumstances, in opposition to the declared sense of the country, has been passed a measure, imposing on the people a new Constitution, and subverting the old one."

"The Ministers," says Mr Lecky, "by money or by dignities had bought almost all the great borough owners as well as a large proportion of the Members, and they thus made their success certain. One difficulty, however, still remained. It was found that several of the borough Members were not prepared to vote for the Union, although their patrons had been bought. The most obvious way of meeting this difficulty would

[1] Woodfall's "Parliamentary Debates," ii. p. 370.   [2] *Ibid.*, ii. p. 399.

Some Means by which the Union was carried. 105

have been to have dissolved Parliament, but such a step would have given the free constituencies an opportunity of testifying their abhorrence of the measure."[1] There were, as I have said, only 128 Members returned by a semblance of popular choice. If they had all voted against the Union, their collective vote would not have affected the result. It would, however, have refuted the calumny of the Ministers that the Irish people desired the Union.

We learn from a letter of Lord Cornwallis to the Duke of Portland, that on the 13th March 1800, Sir John Parnell moved, "That an address be presented to His Majesty, to request His Majesty would dissolve the present Parliament, and call a new one before the present measure of Legislative Union should be concluded." The motion was of course opposed by the Government and defeated. The concluding sentence of this letter is, I think, not without significance. "The Martial-Law Bill was read a third time and passed."[2]

3. *Compensation to Patrons of Nomination Boroughs.*

"Of the 300 Members of the Irish Parliament, 172 were," says Mr Butt, "absolutely the nominees either of the English Government or of persons who held the power of nomination as their private property—in some instances of English noblemen—in many instances of absentee proprietors; in four instances at least of the Bishops of the Irish Established Church, not of Irish Bishops, but of Bishops sent here to serve the English interest, like Cleaver at Kilkenny, or Boulter and Stone at Armagh. The records or the awards of compensation to private proprietors for boroughs extinguished at the Union abundantly establish these facts.

---

[1] "Leaders of Public Opinion," p. 180.
[2] March 14, 1880. "Cornwallis Correspondence," iii. pp. 212, 213.

Eighty-four boroughs were treated as private property, and compensation given for that property to their patrons.[1]"

Each seat was valued at £7500, and the whole sum awarded as compensation amounted to £1,260,000.[2]

It is, I think, instructive to observe this idea of compensation attaining definite shape in the minds of the promoters of the Union. Thus, two days after the defeat of the measure in the Irish House of Commons on its first introduction, Lord Cornwallis writes a "secret and confidential" letter to the Duke of Portland. He observes that the proposal of the Union provoked the enmity of the "borough-mongers," and others, but "certainly had not affected the nation at large," and was not "disagreeable to Catholic or Protestant dissenters," and further on says, "The late experiment has shown the impossibility of carrying a measure which is contrary to the private interests of those who are to decide upon it, and which is not supported by the voice of the country at large."[3] Having thus stated his private opinion of the feeling of the country on a measure which Mr Pitt four days later described in the English House of Commons as a Union "by free consent, and on just and equal terms," in due course means are devised for satisfying private interests. "I have no difficulty," writes the Duke of Portland, in another "secret and confidential" letter, dated March 8, 1799, "in authorising your Excellency to hold out the idea of compensation to all persons possessed of that species of property (nomination boroughs), and I do not scruple to advise

---

[1] "Proceedings of the Home Rule Conference, 1873," pp. 7, 8.
[2] "Cornwallis Correspondence," iii. p. 323.
[3] The letter thus concludes immediately afterwards: "I think it is evident if ever a second trial of the Union is to be made the Catholics must be included." "Cornwallis Correspondence," iii. p. 52.

that the compensation should be made on a liberal principle."[1]

At the same time the idea struck them that so glaring a perversion of public trusts for private benefit might form in itself an irrefragable argument for Parliamentary Reform. "Government," it is stated in the "Project for the Representation of Ireland in the Imperial Parliament," which is apparently the work of Lord Castlereagh, is unwilling to make any admission which might found an argument for Parliamentary Reform, by making it a general principle of the arrangement to strike off the close boroughs, and keep those only

---

[1] Portland to Cornwallis. The Duke does not admit Lord Castlereagh's valuation of English or Irish boroughs. "Castlereagh Correspondence," ii. p. 204. Lord Brabourne differs in opinion from the Duke of Portland, who advises compensation to the borough proprietors, and whose motives for so doing are, I think, clear, having regard to the letter of Lord Cornwallis. "These compensations," Lord Brabourne writes, "may have been right or wrong, but it must be remembered that they were indiscriminately paid to the opponents and supporters of the Act of Union, and cannot therefore be described as bribes for support" ("Facts and Fictions in Irish History," p. 30). The recommendation of the Duke of Portland that the "compensation should be on a liberal principle," and a remark of Lord Brabourne's with reference to what he terms "the bestowal of places and honours," that "there was every wish and intention to conciliate Irish national feeling, and to meet with a liberal response every individual claim that might be advanced" (*Ibid.*, p. 29), would provoke a smile were it not for the solemnity of the issue. "Irish national feeling" was to be conciliated at the expense of the people of Ireland. The "liberal response" was to come from the starving Irish poor. Ireland was taxed with every farthing of the expenses occasioned by what Lord Castlereagh himself has termed the "profligacy of the means" whereby the Union was carried. In 1799 the Irish National debt was only fourteen millions, at the time of the Union it had mounted to twenty-one millions, the country being charged with the bribes for which her liberty was bought and sold. The generosity of the contrivers of the Union with the money of the land they were degrading reminds one of the generosity of

> Sir Agmondisham Vesey, who out of his bounty
> Built a fine bridge—at the cost of the county."

which are open." ¹ This suggestion was adopted. Out of the thirty-four boroughs which continued to return Members after the Union, the editor of the "Cornwallis Correspondence" tells us that twelve only "were really open." ²

Lord Cornwallis himself thinks the compensation to "borough-mongers" to be a rift in the Union lute. "The subject of giving compensation to boroughs is," he writes, "obviously the most exceptionable in the present arrangement, and they (the Opposition) will of course endeavour to make an impression by debating this principle." ³

"You have adopted," said Mr Plunket in the Irish House of Commons on the 15th January 1800, "the extremes of the despot and the revolutionist; you have invoked the loyal people and Parliament of Ireland, who were not calling on you; you have essayed every means to corrupt that Parliament, if you could, to sell their country; you have exhausted the whole patronage of the Crown in the execution of that system, and to crown all, you openly avow, and it is notoriously a part of your plan, that the constitution of Ireland is to be purchased for a stipulated sum. I state a fact for which, if untrue, I deserve serious reprehension. I state it as a fact, which you cannot dare to deny, that £15,000 a-piece is to be given to certain individuals as the price for their surrendering—what? Their property?

[1] "Castlereagh Correspondence," iii. p. 56.
[2] "Cornwallis Correspondence," iii. p. 234. "By setting the price of £15,000 on each Irish borough which was to be disfranchised, the strongest colour was given to the assertion of Reformers that the boroughs of this country (England) were likewise bought and sold."—Dr Lawrence, May 2, 1800. Woodfall's "Parliamentary Debates," ii. p. 594.
[3] Cornwallis to Portland, March 11, 1800. "Cornwallis Correspondence," iii. p. 211.

No; but the rights of the representation of the people of Ireland; and you will then proceed in this or in an Imperial Parliament to lay taxes on the wretched natives of this land to pay the purchase of their own slavery. It was in the last stage of vice and decrepitude that the Roman purple was set up for sale, and the sceptre of the world transferred for a stipulated price; but, even then, the horde of slaves who were to be ruled would not have endured that their country itself should have been enslaved to another nation."[1]

"What," asked Mr Plunket on the 10th March 1800, "What will the people of Ireland say to so base and flagitious a piece of plunder as this juggling from them by taxes on their wants and miseries the enormous sum of a million and a-half to reward the betrayers of their rights and liberties."[2]

The protest of the Lords against the Union is on this point no less emphatic. "Because, when we advert to the corrupt and unconstitutional language held out by the Minister to such Members as claimed property in boroughs, intimating to them that they should be considered as their private property, and should be purchased as such, and the price paid out of the public purse; such language appears to us to amount to a proposal to buy the Irish Parliament for Government, and makes the Union a measure of bargain and sale between the Minister and the individual."

The language in the English Parliament on this subject was equally plain. Thus Mr Johns stated that Mr Pitt "was determined to carry his point, and said to himself—

'Si nequeo Superos Acheronta movebo;'

[1] "Plunket's Life," i. pp. 189, 190.   [2] *Ibid.*, i. p. 196.

and he moved Acheron with a vengeance." "He (Mr Johns) reprobated the idea that had been held out in this transaction that the boroughs were a marketable commodity, and that the people were to pay for those very boroughs, the members for which voted away their own existence as legislators, with the rights, privileges, and independence of the Irish people."[1]

4. *Sale of Peerages.*

"Another mode of corruption," says Mr Lecky, "scarcely less efficacious (than that of compensation to the borough-mongers) was employed to influence the wealthier Irish gentry. Peerages to this class are always a peculiar object of ambition, and they had long been given in Ireland with a lavishness which materially degraded the position. In England the simultaneous creation of twelve peers by Harley had been regarded as a scandalous and unprecedented straining of the prerogative; but no sooner had the Union been carried than Lord Cornwallis sent to England the names of sixteen persons to whom he had expressly promised Irish peerages as rewards for their support of the Union. But these promotions were but a small part of what was found necessary. Twenty-two Irish peers were created, five peers received English peerages, and twenty peers received higher titles."[2]

The full list of these "honours" is reproduced in the "Cornwallis Correspondence."[3]

The circumstances attending the creation of the sixteen peerages, alluded to by Mr Lecky, are curious. The patents are all dated the 30th July 1800, the day

---

[1] Woodfall's "Parliamentary Debates," ii. p. 382.
[2] "Leaders of Public Opinion," p. 179.
[3] "Cornwallis Correspondence," iii. pp. 318, 319.

but one before the Union Bill received the Royal assent. The Irish peers were to be represented in the House of Lords by twenty-eight of their own number, elected by them for life. The British Cabinet assented to Lord Cornwallis' suggestion, but at first declined to grant the patents for these peerages till after the election of representative peers had taken place.

The correspondence between the Irish Lord-Lieutenant and his Secretary and the authorities in England so clearly illustrates the sentiments and views of the authors of the Union on the means and the men by which that measure was carried, that I shall be justified in quoting it copiously. It is also noteworthy, as it shows that the chief promoters of this measure in their dealings, even with each other, were lacking in the conventional "honour amongst thieves."

The Duke of Portland thus intimates to Lord Cornwallis the polite refusal of the English Cabinet to allow the sixteen to take part in the election of representative peers:—"Your Excellency appears to have been well aware of the manner in which his Majesty would naturally receive a proposal for so large an addition to the peerage, by the statement you have made of the considerations which you hope may dispose his Majesty to assent to such a measure, and I have the satisfaction of acquainting your Excellency that the proceeding has been attended with the happiest effect, for the sense his Majesty is graciously pleased to entertain of the ability with which you have overcome the difficulties you have had to struggle with, and of the judgment you have displayed in administering the government of the kingdom of Ireland, have given such a weight to your representations in favour of the gentlemen you have recommended for this high mark of his Majesty's favour, that I am commanded to signify to you his Majesty's determination to accede to your request. At the same time I am particularly directed to let you know that his Majesty will very unwillingly consent to the conferring of any of these intended honours till after the election of the peers has taken place; and he, therefore, relies upon the exertion of your Excellency's utmost influence, and depends much upon the confidence which your conduct has so justly entitled you to from the candidates for those distinctions, as well as from the country at large, to reconcile them to their being suspended till after the accomplishment of that event, with the exceptions, however, of the promotions of Viscounts O'Neill and Bandon, for which the necessary letters will be sent to your Excellency as soon as you will signify your wishes for them, as well as for conferring the vacant ribbon of the Order of St Patrick on the Earl of Altamont, which his Majesty very much approves."[1]

Lord Cornwallis was bitten, and severely bitten, by the asp which lurked in this epistolary bouquet. "In the most severe trials," he says, "I have hitherto been able to conduct myself with a firmness becoming a man of honour and integrity, but now my condition is so much altered that I must either say to those I am about to disappoint, that I will not keep my word with them or acknowledge that I have pretended to have power which I did not possess, and that I must declare my engagements to be void because his Majesty's Ministers have refused to fulfil them." "I am so overcome by your Grace's letter that I know not how to proceed." The letter concludes with a wish that the King, in the event of the royal consent being withheld, "would be pleased to allow him to retire from a station which he

---

[1] June 12, 1800. "Castlereagh Correspondence," iii. p. 321.

could not hold with honour to himself, or with any prospect of advantage to his (the King's) service."[1]

Lord Castlereagh considers his "*character*" to be involved. He writes to Lord Camden the day after that on which Lord Cornwallis' letter was written :—" If the Irish Government is not enabled to keep faith with the various individuals who have acted upon a principle of confidence in their honour, it is morally impossible, my dear Lord, that either Lord Cornwallis or I can remain in our present situations; the moment it is surmised that we have lost the confidence and support of the English Government, we shall have every expectant upon our backs, and it will remain a breach of faith as injurious to the character of the Government as to our own, having given an assurance which we were not enabled to fulfil."[2] Again, writing from Dublin to Mr Cooke, on the 21st June 1800, Lord Castlereagh says: "They sent him (Lord Cornwallis) into this country to risk an established character at the close of a political life, and I cannot easily persuade myself that Mr Pitt will give him up on a point of patronage after what he has accomplished. But from King's arguments, it appears that the Cabinet, after having carried the measure by the force of influence of which they were apprised in every despatch sent from hence for the last eighteen months, wish to forget all this, they turn short round and say it would be a pity to tarnish all that has been so well done by giving any such shock to the public sentiment. If they imagine they can take up popular grounds by disappointing their supporters, and by dis-

---

[1] June 17, 1800. "Secret and Confidential." "Castlereagh Correspondence," iii. p. 326.

[2] June 18, 1800. "Secret." "Castlereagh Correspondence," iii. p. 327.

gracing the Irish Government, I think they will find themselves mistaken; it will be no secret what has been promised, or by what means the Union has been secured. Disappointment will encourage, not prevent, disclosure, and the only effect of such a proceeding on their part will be to add the weight of their testimony to that of the anti-Unionists in proclaiming the profligacy of the means by which the measure has been accomplished." This Mr Cooke, to whom Lord Castlereagh thus wrote, was the gentleman from whose " Notes on the Union" I have previously quoted. He was author of a Government pamphlet on the Union which appeared in 1798. He was, as I have said, one of the direct agents in the bribery system. An Englishman by birth, he had no connection whatever with Ireland, in whose Parliament he sat for a nomination borough. One of Lord Fitzwilliam's first acts in 1795 was the dismissal of this gentleman with a retiring pension of £1200 per annum. He wished the Castle officials to be "clerks, not ministers." Mr Cooke was instantly reinstated by Lord Camden, who, as we shall see, corresponded with him on this interesting subject. In the same letter from which I have quoted, Lord Castlereagh pleads in justification of the immediate creation of the sixteen peerages,—" They are all granted either to persons actually members of, or connected with, the House of Commons. The only question is, if the Peerages are to be granted, whether in policy or upon constitutional grounds we are called upon to forego their support in the elections by postponing their creation till after the Union passes. My own feeling has always been that upon the latter grounds it is due to them to give them a participation in the elections."[1]

[1] June 21, 1800. "Secret." "Castlereagh Correspondence," iii. pp. 330-332.

Lord Camden is greatly concerned in the question of these creations. "I imagine," he writes to Mr Cooke, "they will all be assented to, though Sir J. B.'s creation and representation is almost intolerable."[1]

The tragedy which a refusal would have entailed was, however, averted; here is a cheering message from Mr Cooke to Lord Castlereagh,—"I think you ought to send over the official recommendations of the Peerages without a moment's delay."[2] "I am satisfied," says Lord Castlereagh, writing to Mr Cooke, June 25, 1800, "the Union would not have been carried without the most unqualified authority in the person charged with its execution, the most entire support from the English Government, which, perhaps, a variance of opinions on points viewed under dissimilar circumstances hardly admits; and lastly a power to act without delay and with the utmost secresy."[3]

The Sir J. B. to whom Lord Camden alludes, is Sir John Blaquiere. The expressions of Lord Camden with regard to Sir J. Blaquiere, and the other references to him which I am about to quote, seem somewhat inconsistent with the encomiums bestowed on the sixteen by the Duke of Portland. "Blaquiere's business has been very unpleasant. I succeeded yesterday in a final adjustment with him to the satisfaction of all parties. He played the true black in the business, but, all things considered, we have got well out of it. Some of our Swiss guards are pressing us hard."[4] "You have probably heard," writes Lord Castlereagh to Mr Cooke, "from Marsden that Blaquiere has waived his

[1] June 22, 1800. "Castlereagh Correspondence," iii. 334.
[2] June 23, 1800. "Castlereagh Correspondence," iii. p. 335.
[3] "Secret." "Castlereagh Correspondence," iii. p. 337.
[4] Marsden to Cooke, July 10, 1800. "Private." "Cornwallis Correspondence," iii. p. 276.

Representative Peerage for *more substantial* objects."[1] The editor of the "Cornwallis' Correspondence" informs us that those objects were a pension of £1000 per annum. He had previously obtained compensation for his sinecures, which amounted to £3200 per annum.[2] The creation of sixteen new Peers was no doubt lavish, still Lord Cornwallis acted within the powers expressly conferred on him by the Government *before* the Union was virtually carried.

"He (Mr Pitt) consented to *eighteen* new Peers, and did not absolutely limit us to that number, although our conduct has been reprobated for sending over a list of sixteen, one of which is a Barony to Lord Montrath, with the remainder to Mr Coote, and two are female Peerages."[3]

5. *The Bribing of Members of the Irish House of Commons.*

The dismissals, the abuse of the Place Bill, the compensation to borough owners, the sale of the peerage, present a picture sufficiently gloomy but not so dark as the reality. The House of Commons was assailed by direct metallic corruption. "Grattan," says Mr

---

[1] July 12, 1800. "Secret." "Cornwallis Correspondence," iii. p. 278.

[2] Lord Brabourne cites both Lord Castlereagh and Sir J. Blaquiere as witnesses on the question of corruption. Their testimony can be placed at its true value in the face of the documents from which I have quoted. "But what," Lord Brabourne innocently asks, "with regard to the bestowal of places and honours? Lord Castlereagh, Sir J. Blaquiere, Lord Hawkesley, and others in their places in Parliament strongly denied the charges of corruption. Still there can be no doubt that peerages and places were promised and given which would not have been bestowed if the recipients had not supported the measure of the Government ("Facts and Fictions in Irish History," pp. 28, 29). I would be glad to know whether Lord Brabourne thinks that Lord Castlereagh and Sir J. Blaquiere were stating what they believed to be true, or even what they did not know to be false, when from their places in Parliament they, as his Lordship tells us, "strongly denied the charges of corruption."

[3] Cornwallis to Ross, July 11, 1880, "Correspondence," iii. p. 277.

Some Means by which the Union was carried. 117

Lecky, "who had unusual opportunities of judging, afterwards expressed his opinion that of the Members who voted for the Union only seven were unbribed."[1] Mr Hardy, who sat in the three last Irish Parliaments, refrained from writing the story of the Union, and confined himself to the Biography of Lord Charlemont, who died in 1799, giving as his reason that he did not care to bequeath enmities to his children, and that but seven of those who composed the majority in favour of the Union were unbribed.[2] Mr O'Connell stated without fear of contradiction, when defending himself in the State trials before a jury composed exclusively of Unionists: "You know that there were one million two hundred and seventy-five thousand pounds actually spent in the purchase of rotten burghs. You know that there were near three millions besides expended in actual payment of the persons who voted for the Union."[3]

The secret correspondence of the promoters of the Union proves that they coincided with its opponents in the opinion that the measure was contrary to the sense of the Parliament by which it was actually passed. "We have," says Lord Cornwallis, "a lukewarm, and in some instances, an unwilling majority. The enemy have a bold and deeply-interested minority, which will, I am afraid, even after our own friends are reckoned, run us much nearer than most people expect."[4] Again, five weeks later, Lord Cornwallis writes to the same correspondent: "God only knows how the business

[1] "Leaders of Public Opinion," p. 181.
[2] "Grattan's Life," v. p. 113.   [3] "R. v. O'Connell," p. 628.
[4] "It is a sad thing to be forced to manage knaves, but it is ten times worse to deal with fools. Between the one and the other, I entertain every day more doubt of our success on the great question of the Union." Cornwallis to Ross, Dec. 28, 1799. "Private." "Cornwallis Correspondence," iii. p. 153.

will terminate, but it is so hard to struggle against private interests and the pride and prejudices of a nation, that I shall never feel confident of success until the Union is actually carried."[1] "I hope we shall be able to keep our friends true," says Lord Castlereagh to Mr King in a letter soliciting money to be expended in bribery; "a few votes might have a very injurious effect."[2] On the 18th April 1800, Lord Cornwallis writes to General Ross: "The nearer the great event approaches the more are the needy and interested senators alarmed at the effects it may possibly have on their interests and the provision for their families, and I believe that *half of our majority* would be at least as much delighted as any of our opponents if the measure could be defeated."[3] These are the sentiments of the

[1] Cornwallis to Ross, Feb. 4, 1800. "Cornwallis Correspondence," iii. p. 177.

[2] Feb. 27, 1800. "Private and Secret." "Cornwallis Correspondence," iii. p. 200, 201.

[3] "Cornwallis Correspondence," iii. p. 228. Here again Lord Brabourne differs from Lord Cornwallis and Lord Castlereagh, who, it must be admitted, knew something about the matter. "It may have been," says Lord Brabourne, "and probably was the case, that many Irishmen, believing the Union to be desirable, and being, therefore, willing to support it, deemed it at the same time allowable to make the best bargain they could for themselves, and obtain as high 'a compensation' as possible for their loss of place or position. Their conduct is, of course, to be condemned, but it is a very different thing from the charge of having believed the Union to be injurious to their country and to have sacrificed her interests by the sale of their votes. I am not attempting to deny that bargains were made and corruption practised in order to secure the passing of the Union, but I maintain that there has been an immense amount of exaggeration upon the subject, and that the British government of the day found so much corruption in the system previously existing in Ireland that they were almost forced to fight 'fire by fire.'"—"Facts and Fictions in Irish History," pp. 29, 30. See also a very ingenious argument to the same effect by Dr Webb, Q.C. "There never was a sterner moralist than Hallam, yet Hallam distinguishes between the case of a man who takes a bribe to betray his principles, and the case of a man who accepts a gratification to promote them."—"Irish Question," p. 39.

statesmen of the Union on the popularity of the measure they were forcing on the Irish Parliament with the strong arm. The views of the opponents of this transaction are precisely similar. "If," says Mr Bushe, in the Irish House of Commons, "posterity were to believe that human frailty and human necessities were so practised on, that the private sentiments and public conduct of several could not be reconciled, and that when the Minister could influence twenty votes, he could not command one 'Hear him.' I say not that these things are so, but I ask you, if your posterity believe them to be so, will posterity validate this transaction, or will they feel themselves bound to do so? I answer, when a transaction, though fortified by a seven-fold form, is radically fraudulent, that all the forms and solemnities of law are but so many badges of the fraud, and posterity, like a great court of conscience, will pronounce its judgment."[1]

It was one of the provisions of the Act of Union, that only twenty placemen should sit for Irish constituencies. Mr Plunket thus comments on this arrangement: "Into a British Parliament only twenty men will be admitted of that description which now constitutes the Minister's majority. Let no more than twenty placemen vote on the present question, and I would freely and cheerfully submit the fate of the country to their decision. Let the Minister even retain all his placemen, and let him put the question of Ireland to a ballot, and I will abide the issue. Let the gentlemen who hold places vote uninfluenced by the fear of losing their situations, and even they will act like Irishmen. Who, then, are this body of

[1] "Plunket's Life," ii. p. 366. "The miserable tale," says Professor Dicey, "of the transactions which carried the Treaty of Union, teaches at least one indisputable lesson—the due observance of legal formalities will not induce a people to pardon what they deem to be acts of tyranny, made all the more hateful by their combination with deceit."—"Case of England against Home Rule," p. 251.

men to whose opinion we are asked to look up with so much reverence? They are men whom a British Minister has declared too foul to pollute the walls of a British senate. Those men who are too base to enter the door of one Parliament, are to vote the extinction of another and decide for ever upon the liberties of the country."[1]

"When," says Mr Grey, in the English House of Commons, "I consider the majority who voted with the Minister, I must say, that if left to itself untempted, unawed, unintimidated, it (the Irish Parliament) would, without hesitation, have rejected the resolutions (in favour of the Union). There are 300 Members in all, and 120 of these strenuously opposed the measure, among whom were two-thirds of the county Members, the representatives of the city of Dublin, and of almost all the towns which it is proposed shall send Members to the Imperial Parliament; 162 voted in favour of the Union, of these 116 were placemen, some of them English generals on the staff without one foot of ground in Ireland, and completely dependent upon Government.[2] Is there any ground to presume that even the Parliament of Ireland thinks as the right hon. gentleman (Mr Pitt) supposes, or that, acting only from a regard to the good of their country, the Members would not have reprobated the measure as strongly and unanimously as the rest of the people?" "I defy any man to lay his hand upon his heart and say that he believes the Parliament of Ireland was sincerely in favour of the measure. We are to receive an hundred Irish Members into the House of Commons, and these, the right hon. gentleman says, will be suffi-

---

[1] "Plunket's Life," i. p. 197.

[2] Mr Grey said, in the progress of the debate, that this observation very particularly applied to General Lake, the Commander of the Forces.

cient to express the will and support the interests of the Irish nation. By the vote of these the Union would have been rejected, as almost all the Members for the counties and towns by which they are to be chosen keenly oppose it. Thus on the right hon. gentleman's own ground his assertion is refuted." [1]

6. *The stifling and falsification of public opinion.*

A few days after the rejection of the measure of Legislative Union by the Irish Parliament, in January 1799, the Duke of Portland writes to Lord Castlereagh on the *constitutional aspect* of the question. "I have seen," he says, "with some surprise, as well as with real concern, a deference expressed for the opinion of constituents, which I conceive to have been as unnecessary as it is certainly unconstitutional, and in cases where the representative might have taken the lead and taught his constituents the manner in which they were to consider the effects of this measure." [2] When, however, the Members proved recalcitrant the promoters of the Union changed their minds, and considered it advisable to make a pretence of eliciting the public sentiment on the measure. "I am preparing," Lord Cornwallis writes to General Ross, "to set out on a tour for three weeks to the south, for the purpose of obtaining declarations, &c., in favour of the Union." [3] I will relate the nature and effects of this progress in the burning words of Mr Plunket, speaking in the Irish House of Commons on the 16th January 1800. "The representative of Majesty sets out on his mission to court the sovereign majesty of the people. It is painful to dwell on that disgraceful expedition. No place too obscure to be visited—no rank too

---

[1] Woodfall's "Parliamentary Debates," ii. pp. 398, 399.
[2] January 29, 1799. "Castlereagh Correspondence," ii. p. 146.
[3] Ju y 21, 1799. "Cornwallis Correspondence," iii. p. 118.

low to be courted—no threat too vile to be employed—the counties not sought to be legally convened by their sheriffs—no attempt to collect the unbiassed suffrage of the intelligent and independent part of the community—public addresses begged for from petty villages, and private signatures smuggled from public counties. And how procured? By the influence of absentee landlords, not over the affections, but over the terrors of their tenantry; by griping agents and revenue officers. And after all this mummery had been exhausted, after the lustre of royalty had been tarnished by this vulgar intercourse with the lowest of the rabble; after every spot had been selected where a paltry address could be procured, and every place avoided where a manly sentiment could be encountered; after abusing the names of the dead and forging the signatures of the living; after polling the inhabitants of the gaol, and calling out against Parliament the suffrages of those who dare not come in to sign them till they had got their protection in their pocket; after employing the revenue officer to threaten the publican that he should be marked as a victim, and the agent to terrify the shivering tenant with the prospect of his turf-bog being withheld if he did not sign your addresses; after employing your military commanders, the uncontrolled arbiters of life and death, to hunt the rabble against the constituted authorities;—after squeezing the lowest dregs of a population of near five millions, you obtained about five thousand signatures, three-fourths of whom affixed their names in surprise, terror, or total ignorance of the subject."[1] The Protest and Address to the King, moved in the Irish House of Commons by Lord Corry, accuses the Ministers of "abetting and encourag-

[1] "Plunket's Life," i. pp. 187, 188.

ing the using of various arts and stratagems to procure from individuals of the lowest order, some of whom were their prisoners and felons, scandalous signatures against the Constitution."[1]

Mr Pitt seems to have laid much stress on these petitions. Thus, in a letter from Mr Cooke to Lord Castlereagh, marked "secret," and dated 5th April 1800, we find this statement :—" He (Mr Pitt) is anxious that if there be a run of petitions to the King against Union, counter-declarations should be renewed, if you saw it could be done with success. He is afraid that if the petitions should become very numerous, and not be counteracted, an impression will be made as to the sense of the people being against the measure. He wishes much for counter-declarations from our friends."[2] Mr Pitt was in this instance doomed to disappointment. A few weeks after that letter was written, Mr Grey, speaking in the English House of Commons, proved conclusively that "the sense of the people" was against the measure. "It is stated," he said, "in the speech of the Lord-Lieutenant to the Irish Parliament, and more clearly and positively in the speech of the Minister, that five-sevenths of the country, and all the principal commercial towns, except Dublin, had petitioned in favour of the Union. This statement I controvert, and shall disprove. The way in which it is attempted to be made out that five-sevenths of the country had petitioned for the Union, is by saying that nineteen counties had, and that these counties constitute five-sevenths of the surface of Ireland. That petitions were presented from several different counties I will not deny ; but by what means are they obtained, and by whom are they signed ? The Lord-Lieutenant, who

[1] R. v. O'Connell, p. 529.
[2] "Castlereagh Correspondence," iii. pp. 260, 261.

besides being the chief civil magistrate in the kingdom, is commander of a disciplined army of 170,000 men, who is able to proclaim martial law when he pleases, and can subject whom he pleases to the arbitrary trial of a court-martial, in his progress through the kingdom procured these petitions, which are signed by a few names, and those by no means the most respectable. It has been said that all were Jacobins who opposed the Union. It might be said with more truth that a great proportion of those who signed these vaunted petitions in favour of it were men in the power of the Lord-Lieutenant, and who were obliged, from the fear of punishment, to come forward and put down their names. These petitions, besides, disrespectable as they are, were clandestinely obtained: not one of them was voted at a meeting called together by the High Sheriff, legally constituted, of which there was a reasonable notice. They can with no propriety be called the petitions of counties; they are merely those of a few worthless individuals. Yet the right honourable gentleman (Mr Pitt) tells us that they prove the whole Irish nation to be decidedly in favour of the measure. Of this species of groundless declamation, however, he has not the honour of being the original inventor. We have an admirable instance of it in our great dramatic poet. The Duke of Buckingham, in giving Richard III. an account of the manner in which the citizens of London had agreed to his claim to the crown, says, after describing the taciturnity and gloominess of the assembly and their seeming dislike to him—

> " Some ten voices cried ' God save King Richard,'
> And then I took 'vantage of those few :
> '.Thanks, gentle citizens and friends,' quoth I ;
> ' This general applause and cheerful shout
> Argues your wisdom and your love to Richard.' "

Some Means by which the Union was carried. 125

Fortunately there were many petitions on the other side—petitions which were not obtained by solicitation and at illegal meetings, but at public assemblies of which legal notice had been given. Twenty-seven counties have petitioned against the measure. The petition from the county of Down is signed by upwards of 17,000 respectable, independent men; and all the others are in similar proportion. Dublin petitioned under the Great Seal of the city, and each of the corporations in it followed the same example. Drogheda petitioned against the Union, and far from Drogheda and Dublin being the only towns which did so, almost every other in the kingdom in like manner testified its disapprobation. Those in favour of the measure possessing great influence in the country obtained a few counter-petitions, and had great opportunities of procuring signatures to these; yet though the petition from Down was signed by 17,000, the counter-petition was signed only by 415. This instance might be taken as a very fair standard for the whole kingdom. Though there were 707,000 who had signed petitions against the measure, the total number of those who declared themselves in favour of it did not exceed 3000, and many of those only prayed that the measure might be discussed. I wish I could have spoken from official information. Had the motion I made for the Lord-Lieutenant of Ireland being directed to transmit all addresses and counter-addresses which have been received [been carried], I should then have this in my power; at present I must speak from private authority, which, however, I believe will be found to be pretty correct. If the facts I state are true, and I challenge any man to falsify one of them, could a nation in more direct terms, or in a more positive way, express its disapprobation of a political measure than Ireland has of a legislative Union with Great Britain ? In fact, the nation is nearly unanimous, and this great majority is composed not of fanatics, bigots, or Jacobins, but of the most respectable in every class in the community." [1]

The expression of public opinion against the Union was suppressed by means as base as those by which petitions in its favour were courted. Thus the Address and Protest to which I have previously referred states that the Ministers endeavoured by their choice of sheriffs to obstruct the regular and constitutional mode whereby the sense of the people had been usually collected ; and this complaint is reiterated by Mr Grattan: "The appointment of Sheriffs to prevent county meetings" forms one of the grounds of the Protest of the Lords against the Union.[2] When the Government were unable by stratagem to prevent county meetings, they resorted to force for the purpose of dispersing such gatherings. "Twenty-seven counties," said Mr Sheridan in the British House of Commons, "had declared against the Union, and with these would have united Antrim and Sligo, if martial law had not been proclaimed and prevented the intended meetings. If the measure was thus to be carried, he had no hesitation in saying that it was an act of tyranny and oppression, and must

[1] April 21, 1800, "Woodfall's Parliamentary Reports," ii. pp. 396-398. Mr Grey estimates the number of signatures to petitions in favour of the Union to amount to 3000. Mr Sheridan in the same debate computes them to be 5000. The larger figure may include the signatures of those who petitioned not for the passing of the Union, but merely for its discussion. Mr Lecky, on the authority of Mr Grattan, states the number of these signatures to be 7000. It is quite clear that Mr Pitt would have produced these petitions if he considered such a proceeding would have helped his cause. Their non-production, when called for by Mr Grey, proves conclusively their worthlessness.

[2] "R. v. O'Connell," p. 529.

become the fatal source of new discontents and future rebellions; and the only standard round which the pride, the passions, and the prejudice of the Irish would rally, was that which would lead them to the recovery of the Constitution that was thus foully and oppressively to be wrested from them." " Martial law, spies, informers, &c., &c., were on all sides marshalled against the opposers of the Union, and then it was only to be wondered how any set of men under such a system of terror would have dared so boldly and manfully to express their abhorrence of it."[1]

"It may be said," says Mr O'Connell, "why did not the Irish people resist the fatal measure? How could they? When the High Sheriff of the Queen's County called a meeting of his bailiwick in the town of Maryborough to petition against the Union, he was met by Colonel Connor with two regiments of infantry and detachments of cavalry and artillery, by whom the meeting was instantly dispersed as the Sheriff was about to take the chair. Again, the High Sheriff of Tipperary convened a meeting of the nobility, gentry, and free-holders of his county; he took the chair, but he had been hardly ten minutes in the court-house when it was filled with armed soldiery, who dispersed the meeting at the point of the bayonet. That was the conduct pursued at this eventful period; corruption, bribery, force, fraud, and terror were used, but still the people of Ireland struggled in every mode they possibly could."[2]

Sir Jonah Barrington gives the following account of the dealings of the Government with public meetings

[1] Woodfall's "Parliamentary Reports," ii. p. 426.
[2] "Report of the Discussion in Dublin Corporation on the Repeal of the Union, 1843," p. 41.

legally convened to protest against the Union:—"Mr Darby, High Sheriff of the King's County, and Major Rogers of the artillery, had gone so far as to place two six-pounders towards the doors of the court-house, where the gentlemen and free-holders of the county were assembling to address as Anti-Unionists, and it is not to be wondered at that the dread of grape shot not only stopped this, but numerous meetings for similar purposes. Yet this was one of the means taken to prevent the expression of public meetings without, and formed a proper comparison for the measures resorted to within the walls of Parliament."[1]

Individuals who made themselves conspicuous in promoting Anti-Union meetings were ruthlessly pursued by the Government. "I myself," says Mr O'Connell, "remember a gentleman from Kerry, Mr St John Mason, who was hunted out of the country, because he dared to put an address into a newspaper, calling on the people of Kerry to petition against the Union— who was pursued to Roscrea, and afterwards committed to Kilmainham gaol, where he lay for months, for no offence but attempting to petition against the Union."[2]

7. *The duping of the Roman Catholics.*

The extracts from the correspondence of Lords Cornwallis and Castlereagh which I have previously cited, prove that the attitude which the Irish Roman Catholics would ultimately adopt on the question of the Union was a matter of intense concern to the Government. A few days after the defeat of the measure in 1799, Lord Cornwallis writes to the Duke of Portland: "I think it evident that if ever a second trial of the Union is to be

---

[1] "Rise and Fall of the Irish Nation," pp. 448, 449.

[2] Report of the "Discussion in Dublin Corporation on the Report of the Union," p. 40.

made, the Catholics must be included."[1] A day or two later, Lord Cornwallis's views on the question assume a definite form. "Were the Catholic question," he says, "to be now carried, the great argument for an Union would be lost, at least as far as the Catholics are concerned. It seems, therefore, incumbent on Government, whatever their inclinations might otherwise be, to prevent its adoption at present."[2] On the 30th January 1799, the Duke of Portland gives Lord Cornwallis specific directions as to the course to be pursued in dealing with this question : "Even if the Opposition try to bribe the Roman Catholics by promising emancipation, the Government is unanimous in opposing it in the Irish Parliament ;] and Lord Cornwallis is to state that whatever the line may be which a Union may enable the United Parliament to adopt, to forward the benevolent intentions of His Majesty towards any part of his subjects,[3] the opposition of Government to any such measure, as with reference to the Irish Parliament separately, must be uniform and exerted to the utmost."[4]

"They (the Catholics)," says Mr Lecky, "were probably aware that the King was hostile to emancipation, but they could not know that both in 1795 and 1798 he had distinctly declared that his objections to it were insuperable, and that the over-

[1] January 26th, 1799. "Secret and Confidential." "Cornwallis Correspondence," iii. p. 52.
[2] January 28th, 1799. Cornwallis to Portland. "Most Secret and Confidential." "Cornwallis Correspondence," iii. p. 55.
[3] Here is the King's own exposition of his "benevolent intentions." "My inclination to the Union with Ireland," he wrote in February 1801, "was chiefly founded on a trust that the uniting of the Established Churches of the two Kingdoms would for ever shut the door to any further measures with respect to the Roman Catholics."—"Leaders of Public Opinion," p. 198.
[4] "Cornwallis Correspondence," iii. p. 59.

tures made to them were made with a perfect knowledge of his sentiments, without any attempt to learn how far they might be modified, or any determination to exert the full ministerial power in their favour. They only knew that the chief Irish representatives of one of the strongest Governments that ever existed in England, represented the Cabinet as unanimously in favour of emancipation, and on that ground solicited their support. Government influence alone had defeated emancipation in 1795. They were told that the Government objection to it would be obviated by a Union, and they inferred that by carrying the Union they were carrying their cause. The great object was to hold out hopes sufficient to secure Catholic support or neutrality, without committing the Government to a distinct pledge; and the end was most dexterously accomplished."[1] Lord Cornwallis was certainly innocent of all participation in this fraud. He was himself a dupe. Writing to General Ross on May 21st, 1800, he says: "You will easily understand that I cannot, either in consideration of my own character or the public safety, leave them (the Roman Catholics) as I found them. I have raised no unauthorised expectations, and have acted throughout with the sanction of the Cabinet."[2] When, after the passing of the Union, he becomes aware of the deception to which he unwittingly contributed, he writes to the same correspondent, and thus, with poignant regret, epitomises the result of his Viceroyalty. "This is a melancholy ending of all my labours."[3]

The artifice was, however, perceived. Thus Mr Bushe,

[1] "Leaders of Public Opinion," pp. 162, 163.
[2] "Cornwallis Correspondence," iii. p. 238.
[3] Ibid., iii. p. 334. "But," he courageously adds, "if the good ship Britannia can weather the storm, I shall be satisfied."

speaking in the Irish Parliament on the 16th January 1800, said:—" If we are to embrace and emancipate our Catholic brethren, shall it be said that the Irish Parliament, which has already relaxed the penal laws till scarcely any remain, is incapable of that liberality? And if it be necessary to reject and refuse the Catholic claims, who is it that will tell the Protestant gentry here assembled in Parliament that they are incompetent to protect themselves? No; a Union is not necessary to do either; but if it be in contemplation to inflame the two sects against each other for the purpose of common subjugation; if some little dirty underhand bargain is to be driven with the Catholic clergy; if the Protestant interest is to be sold to the Catholic or the Catholic to the Protestant; if inconsistent promises are to be held out to each in order to deal impartial treachery to both; then indeed there may be some connection between the two ideas, and as the Rebellion has become an argument for the Union because it has weakened us, so religion becomes an argument for the Union because it has divided us." [1]

[1] "Plunket's Life," ii. p. 364. I do not think that the cry of "the Church in danger," which was, of course, raised by the Government, affected the Protestant community in any appreciable degree. "Clare, Duigenan, and the Bishops, it is true, were ardent advocates of the Union, but it appears tolerably certain that no considerable section of Protestants of any class outside Parliament concurred in their view. The Orangemen were decidedly hostile, and the utmost that could be obtained of them was that they would not act in their corporate capacity in opposition to it. The Established Church has played an important part in the history of the Union, but it was at a much later period."—" Leaders of Public Opinion," p. 165. The article expressing the incorporation of the English and Irish Churches to be a fundamental part of the Union was inserted to gratify Archbishop Agar.—"Cornwallis Correspondence," iii. p. 176. For an interesting account of the doings of this Prelate, see "Leaders of Public Opinion," 157-158, note. He was a high-priest of corruption. The disgraceful record of his career should make Irish Protestants thankful that their Church is now a spiritual, not a political, institution.

Mr Grey, also in the English House of Commons, exposed the ruse. "It is said that the Catholics of Ireland may, on some future occasion, obtain indulgences from the liberality of the United Parliament. It were much to be wished that the Catholics should now be distinctly informed of what advantages they may expect. If the privileges held out to them are sufficient to conciliate their support to the measure so far as they are concerned, my argument would be at an end. I do not see the wisdom of insinuating to them vague hopes of future benefits. They may be induced to conceive expectations which, if disappointed, may produce much serious discontent. Encouraged to entertain sanguine hopes, they may afterwards complain that they have been deceived."[1]

Undoubtedly some Roman Catholic bishops and gentlemen of social position were won over to the cause of the Union by the duplicity of the English Cabinet. The mass of the people were, although dying to obtain emancipation, prepared to spurn it when offered to them, in exchange for the Parliament in College Green. Thus, at the meeting of the Bar to protest against the Union, "Bellew and Lynch, two Catholics, were in the majority; when Grady said the Catholics were for the measure, they denied it, and desired that any opinion should be suspended till a meeting of the Catholics should be held."[2]

[1] Woodfall's "Parliamentary Reports," ii. pp. 404, 405.
[2] Cooke to Castlereagh. "Castlereagh Correspondence," i. p. 344. "At one time he (Lord Cornwallis) hoped to overcome or weaken the opposition by the help of the Catholics, but the Catholics would not listen to his blandishments. They trusted if the separate Parliament were maintained to make their way into it eventually, and though England had saved them from extermination by their Protestant countrymen, yet as long as there was a hope of success they preferred to join the Protestant opposition in defence of their natural independence." "English in Ireland," iii. pp. 549, 550.

Some Means by which the Union was carried. 133

The testimony of Mr O'Connell on this matter is, I think, conclusive. Speaking, in 1843, in the Dublin Corporation, in the discussion on the Repeal of the Union, he said :—" The first time that I ever addressed a public assemblage, when I shuddered at the echo of my own voice, was on the 13th January 1800. That was 'my maiden speech,' and it was made against the Union. I may here observe, by way of parenthesis, as a proof of the resistance that was given by the authorities to the expression of public opinion at the period when the Union was carried; that when we, the Catholics of Dublin, met in the Royal Exchange, in pursuance of advertisements inserted for a fortnight previously in the newspapers, and for the purpose of petitioning against the Union, the chair was scarcely taken when we heard the measured tread of approaching military and Major Sirr entered at the head of a large force of soldiers, who arranged themselves along three sides of the room. Major Sirr called upon the secretary for the resolutions that were to be proposed, and after perusing them twice over, he then graciously permitted us to go on. Undismayed by this interruption, I addressed the meeting ; and I wish to show what my sentiments then were by reading a paragraph from my published speech. I can bear testimony to the accuracy of the report, because I wrote it myself. The original is in the hands of a member of my family. Here is what I said : 'There was another reason why they should come forward as a distinct class—a reason which, he confessed, made the greatest impression upon his feelings. Not content with falsely asserting that the Catholics favoured the extinction of Ireland—this their supposed inclination was attributed to the foulest motives—motives which were the most repugnant to their judgments and most abhorrent to their hearts; it was said that the Catholics were ready to sell their country for a price, or, what was still more depraved, to abandon it on account of the unfortunate animosity which the wretched temper of the times had produced. Can they remain silent under so horrible a calumny? This calumny was flung on the whole body; it was incumbent on the whole body to come forward and contradict it. Yes, they will show every friend of Ireland that the Catholics are incapable of selling their country; they will loudly declare that if their emancipation was offered for their consent to the measure—even were emancipation after the Union a benefit—they would reject it with prompt indignation.' (This sentiment met with loud approbation.) 'Let us,' said he, 'show to Ireland that we have nothing in view but her good— nothing in our hearts but the desire of mutual forgiveness, mutual toleration, and mutual affection; in fine, let every man who feels with me, proclaim that if the alternative were offered him of Union or the re-enactment of the penal code, with all its pristine horrors, that he would prefer without hesitation the latter as the lesser and more sufferable evil. That he would rather confide in the justice of his brethren the Protestants of Ireland, who have already liberated him, than lay his country at the feet of foreigners.' (This sentiment met with much and marked approbation.) I added, 'If there was any man present who could be so far mentally degraded as to consent to the extinction of the liberty, the constitution, and even the name of Ireland, he would call on him not to leave the direction and management of his commerce and property to strangers over whom he had no control.'

"That," said Mr O'Connell, "was my first speech,

and the tenor of my public life shows I have never varied from the sentiments it contains. At the time when the offer was thus made, Mr Foster was making arrangements, which were afterwards betrayed by the Lord-Lieutenant, to have an opposition to the Union followed by the re-enactment of that code and something worse, which I shudder even to think of; and yet, even in that moment, on behalf of my native land, I offered to sacrifice our rights to secure the general interests of our country—confiding, I own, that our Protestant countrymen would not be outdone by us in generosity."[1]

"It was," says Mr Lecky, "an imperious obligation of national honour; it was a matter of vital importance to the future prosperity of the empire, that the Catholics should at this time have been emancipated, and there is no reasonable doubt that Pitt could have carried the measure had he determined it."[2]

8. *The fraud on the Constitution of 1782.*

"If ever," said Mr Bushe in the Irish House of Commons, "there was a solemn 'league and covenant' between nations, the settlement of 1782 is that transaction."

The Duke of Portland, who took such a leading part

---

[1] "Discussion on the Repeal of the Union in Dublin Corporation, 1843," pp. 18, 19. Mr Butt pays this tribute to Mr O'Connell :—" Let me say it with melancholy reverence for his memory, Protestant Ireland has never in this respect done justice to this great Irishman. No man ever lived more opposed to religious intolerance; no man would more strenuously have opposed any sectarian ascendency, or any attempt at political dictation by any spiritual power. No misrepresentation of his character could be more unjust than that which would describe him as the slave of prejudice or bigotry, or the servile adherent of ecclesiastical rule."—"Irish Federalism," p. 107, note.

[2] "Leaders of Public Opinion," p. 199.

[3] "Plunket's Life," ii. p. 362.

in promoting the Union, was Lord-Lieutenant of Ireland in 1782. On the 16th April in that year he thus, as Viceroy, addressed the Irish Parliament:—

"I have it in command from His Majesty to inform this House that His Majesty, being concerned to find that discontents and jealousies are prevailing among his loyal subjects of this country upon matters of great weight and importance, His Majesty recommends to this House to take the same into their serious consideration, in order to such a FINAL ADJUSTMENT as may give mutual satisfaction to his kingdoms of Great Britain and Ireland."

The reply of the House of Commons to this Address contains the following passage:—

"That an humble address be presented to His Majesty to return His Majesty the thanks of this House, signified by His Grace the Lord-Lieutenant, to assure His Majesty of our unshaken attachment to His Majesty's person and Government, and of our lively sense of his paternal care in thus taking the lead to administer content to His Majesty's subjects of Ireland. That thus encouraged by his royal interposition, we shall beg leave, with all duty and affection, to lay before His Majesty the cause of our discontents and jealousies. To assure His Majesty that his subjects of Ireland are a free people. That the crown of Ireland is an imperial crown, inseparably annexed to the crown of Great Britain, on which connection the interests and happiness of both nations essentially depend; but that the kingdom of Ireland is a distinct kingdom, with a Parliament of her own, the sole Legislature thereof. That there is no body of men competent to make laws to bind this nation, except the King, Lords and Commons of Ireland, nor any other Parliament which hath any authority or power

Some Means by which the Union was carried. 137

of any sort whatever in this country, save only the Parliament of Ireland. To assure His Majesty that we humbly conceive that in this right the very essence of our liberty exists, a Right which we, on the part of all the people of Ireland, do claim as their birthright, and which we cannot yield but with our lives."

Mr Pitt, in 1799, endeavoured to argue in the British House of Commons that the arrangement of 1782 was merely a provisional, not a final and determinate settlement of the relations between the Legislatures of the two countries; that in fact the Union was the natural sequence of the very incomplete and hasty plan adopted as a mere temporary contrivance at that time. This theory was refuted by one whose testimony must be regarded as conclusive.

Colonel (afterwards General) Fitzpatrick was Chief Secretary during the Viceroyalty of the Duke of Portland, and, from his official position, intimately acquainted with the features of the settlement of 1782, in whose details and general management he necessarily took a leading part. On the 11th February 1799, he gave the English House of Commons the following narrative of this transaction :—

"He had not the vanity to suppose that any arguments of his could divert the right hon. gentleman (Mr Pitt) from a project on which he seemed to have so much set his mind, and perhaps he might incur censure for what he was going to submit, and yet he hoped that an individual, in a particular situation as he was himself, might be permitted to call the attention of the House. In 1782 he was officially employed in carrying into effect what he would venture to say was then universally considered as a final adjustment between this country and Ireland. He must here remind the

House how the case stood, and he would venture to affirm that if ever there was a compact solemnly entered into and binding between a Prince and State, or between any one State or Kingdom with another binding upon both, the compact of 1782 between England and Ireland was of that character and description, and he could not help thinking that the right hon. gentleman would recollect that many persons, and perhaps the majority of the people of Ireland, thought they did not see it carried into effect until the year 1783, but that they did think they saw it then carried into effect.[1] It might be said that the Union now proposed was not inconsistent with that settlement." "The Union, the Minister says, grows out of the independence of the Parliament of Ireland, that was to say, it grew out of the settlement of 1782 between this country and Ireland. Now, to bring in a measure into one Parliament, and to enter into resolutions upon it, that is to say in the British Parliament, by which the other, that is to say the Irish Parliament, is to surrender (for so it must in some degree) to the other, appeared to him to be totally inconsistent with the independence of the Parliament of Ireland which was established 1782. He would say that the independence of the Parliament of Ireland must disappear after the Union, and that it must be

---

[1] In that year a statute was passed in the British Parliament solemnly renouncing all claims of England to legislate for Ireland, 23 Geo. III., c. 28. See "Irish Parliament, what it was, and what it did," pp. 35-40. In Ireland the arrangement was undoubtedly regarded as final. Thus Lord Mountmorres in his book on the "Transactions of the Irish Parliament," which was published in 1792, and is quoted by Mr Hallam as a standard authority, writes, "The assertion and declaration of the Irish, and the *final renunciation* of the English Parliament in 1783, has established upon an eternal and irrevocable foundation the sole right of their own parliament to legislate for Ireland."

sacrificed before any Union could take place." " He was in Ireland, and had a seat in the House of Commons there when the resolutions passed in 1782. He held at that time an official situation. It was wished at that time to talk them over, which they were very fully after they came into that Assemby. The whole of that Assembly almost was well disposed to these resolutions, but there was one Member of that House, who was afterwards a Member of this, who was not very well disposed to them —he meant Mr Flood. He called on him as an official person in that House to say whether there was any other measure to be grounded on that resolution, to which he answered and assured that gentleman, from the authority of those with whom he acted, there was no constitutional measure to be brought forward—there were some measures to be brought forward on commerce, and he knew not what, but, strictly speaking, there was nothing remaining of a constitutional point to be settled. Surely the Union was a constitutional point, and therefore was so far inconsistent with the settlement of 1782, and which he assured Mr Flood was not to be followed by any measure whatever. This, he assured that gentleman. He would venture to say, that for the fifteen years following this resolution there had been no doubt entertained upon the independence of the Irish Legislature in a constitutional point of view." " He confessed, therefore, he was surprised to hear the right honourable gentleman say anything of a slight nature against the settlement of 1782. He must consider that right honourable gentleman as a party to that settlement. He was a strenuous supporter of the Rockingham Administration; he was a very active Member of Parliament ever since he came into that House." " He would go further, and say it was a settlement which not only had the approbation of the right honourable gentleman, but was a measure that was universally approved of; it had the approbation of many of those who were now the friends and adherents of the right honourable gentleman, some who had been called into another place for changing their political sentiments, while he remained where he was because he had not changed them." " He knew of nothing more violent in all the conduct of the French in point of breach of faith than this measure of the Minister was to the people of Ireland. He should say that he knew of nothing in the conduct of the French that in point of breach of faith was more atrocious than this measure would be towards Ireland if carried in the British Parliament." "The whole was founded on a flagrant breach of faith." "In short, he would say that if this measure had originated in Ireland, the entertaining it here might be fair, but that it should originate in the British Parliament was a thing of which he should never have had any conception if he had not been a witness of the measure." "It was impossible for anything to be more odious than this measure, on account of the breach of faith, without which it was impossible to entertain it for one moment."[1]

Lord Holland expressed himself to the like effect in the British House of Lords : " The impropriety of proposing a violation of the adjustment of 1782 was peculiarly striking at the present hour, when Ireland laboured under so many difficulties ; besides, Ministers were wishing to recall that adjustment at the very moment when the Parliament of Ireland had declared its determination to abide by it." [2]

[1] Feb. 11, 1799, "Parliamentary Register," viii. pp. 11-15, abridged.
[2] March 19, 1799. "Parliamentary Register," viii. p. 305.

Some Means by which the Union was carried. 141

In fact, Lord Minto wrote a pamphlet which was circulated gratuitously by the Government, in which he argued that the constitution of 1782 was obtained by Ireland when England was in *duress*, and ought not accordingly to be respected by England in the day of her power. Mr Bushe thus commented on this matter. He asked his opponent in debate not to "refuse to believe the authority of that disinterested and philanthropic nobleman who has condescended to illuminate the understandings of the Irish nation, and whose authority is so undeniably accredited by the gratuitous circulation of his speech at the expense of the Irish Administration. That noble metaphysician tells you expressly that all those favours were extorted from England at a moment when England was in *duress*. *Duress* is his word; his Lordship seems to have a smattering of forensic phrases, and to have put together a little Scotch law with a little Dutch logic, which, mixed with a good deal of lofty English, has recommended his work to the British Cabinet, because he has had the modesty to *write down* the liberties and characters of Ireland, with, however, the sound discretion of writing those down in another country." "Dominion over Ireland is the legal inheritance of England. Mr Pitt did not cite the injustice of England as a proof of his penitence, but as the title-deed of her power and the monument of her claim. That power, that inheritance was fraudulently conveyed away by *duress* in the year 1782, and the Irish Parliament is now called upon as a great Court of Equity to rip up the fraud and set aside the transaction."[1]

The fraud on the "final adjustment" of 1782 was thus exposed by Mr Plunket in the Irish House of

[1] "Plunket's Life," ii. p. 355.

Commons:—"It is admitted by the Minister that the alleged necessity of Union flows merely from the Constitution of 1782. From Henry II. until that time Great Britain never suggested the idea.[1] It was then suggested not as a measure to be grafted on the constitution, but as a substitute for it. It was found that no man could be hardy enough to utter the sentiment in this country, and it was abandoned.[2] You there-

[1] When, in 1703, and again in 1707, the Irish House of Lords prayed for a Union with England, to rid Ireland of the intolerable burdens to which England's commercial jealousy had subjected her, the proposals were coldly received.—"Castlereagh Correspondence," i. p. 153. See also, Froude's "English in Ireland," i. cap. 11, "First attempt at Union."

[2] Mr Plunket evidently referred to an incident disclosed in the English House of Commons, in the debates in 1799. Stung by General Fitzpatrick's speech, Mr Pitt stated that the arrangement of 1782 was *not* final, and not considered to be final by the Duke of Portland. General Fitzpatrick adhered rigidly to his first statement. Mr Pitt averred that he could by documentary evidence convince him of his error, and offered to show him the documents. The General, who probably knew Mr Pitt, declined any confidences, on the ground that there could be no judges between them. Mr Pitt then consented, in the event of General Fitzpatrick, on the perusal of these documents, adhering to his opinion, to produce them to the House. They consisted of seven letters, the first dated 6th May 1782, and the last, 22d June in that year. From them it appears that the Duke of Portland was, at the moment of its birth, endeavouring to strangle the Parliamentary liberty of Ireland. Here are two extracts from this correspondence. Writing to Lord Shelburne, on the 6th June 1782, the Duke of Portland says :—" I shall acquaint your Lordship that I have reason to hope that I may be shortly enabled to lay before you the sketch or outlines of an Act of Parliament, to be adopted by the Legislatures of the respective kingdoms, by which the superintending power and supremacy of Great Britain in all matters of State and general commerce will be virtually and effectually acknowledged," and so on. On the 22d June the Duke writes to Lord Shelburne :— "The disappointment and mortification I suffer by the unexpected change in these dispositions, which had authorised me to entertain the hopes I had perhaps too sanguinely expressed in the letter which I had the honour of writing to your Lordship the 6th instant, must not prevent my acquainting you that for the present these expectations must be given up." The letter concludes with the statement that "any attempt to conciliate the

upon acknowledged our independent constitution, and said that all grounds of constitutional disagreement between the two countries were thereby for ever precluded; and yet you now tell us that thereby, and thereby only, they were created. In 1785 commercial differences arose; there were long negotiations between the two countries, yet the name of Union never hinted at.[1] They were broken off, still Union never hinted at. At a later period they were renewed and settled, and still Union never hinted at; in 1789 the question of Regency arose, and Union was never hinted at.[2] And it is worthy of remark that at these latter

minds of this nation to any such measure as I intimated the hope of, would at this moment be delusive and impossible." The correspondence vindicated General Fitzpatrick's accuracy (see "Parliamentary Register," viii. pp. 535-541). The letters were written in 1782, the Act of Renunciation passed in 1783. The part taken by the Duke of Portland in the corruption of the Irish Parliament is manifest. Lord Stanhope, however, whom Lord Brabourne quotes with approval, credits the Duke with high feeling and unblemished honour. "Facts and Fictions in Irish History," p. 22.

[1] The Union *was* hinted at in 1785. The Duke of Rutland was then Lord-Lieutenant. Speaking in the British House of Lords on 11th April 1799, the Bishop of Llandaff made this remarkable statement: "In writing to the Duke of Rutland about that time (1785), I perfectly well remember having said, 'You and your friend the Minister of England would immortalise your characters if, instead of a mere commercial arrangement, you could accomplish by honourable means and on equitable terms, a legislative Union between the two kingdoms.' His answer to this suggestion was so singular that I shall never forget it. It was to this effect: he wholly approved of the measure, but added, the man who should attempt to carry the measure into execution would be tarred and feathered."— "Parliamentary Register," viii. p. 361.

[2] It has always been an acknowledged principle of the Irish Constitution, that whoever is king *de facto* of England is king *de jure* in Ireland. In 1789, on the occasion of the first mental derangement of George III., the British Parliament conferred the Regency on the Prince of Wales, with limited powers. The Irish Parliament, adopting the views of Mr Fox and the Whig party in the British House of Commons, called on him, by address, to assume the full powers of the Crown. "There can be no doubt," says Lord Brougham, "that Mr Fox's opinions in 1788 were far more in accordance, than those of Mr Pitt, with the spirit of a constitution

periods both countries were in profound peace, foreign and domestic, and nothing existed to prevent the fair sense of every man in the kingdom, in or out of Parliament, being had upon the subject. At last, in 1795, we see the measure peeping out of the British Cabinet, and the propriety of its adoption mentioned as the reason for dashing the hope that had been held out to the Catholic."[1]

The ninth reason in the Protest of the Irish Lords against the Union runs thus:—

"Because we consider the intended Union a direct breach of trust, not only by the Parliament with the people, but by the Parliament of Great Britain with that of Ireland—inasmuch as the tenor and purport of the settlement of 1782 did intentionally and expressly exclude the reagitation of constitutional principles between the two countries, and did establish the exclusive legislative authority of the Irish Parliament which abhors all approach to election in the appointment of a Chief Magistrate."—"British Constitution," p. 263. The king's recovery terminated the dispute. This collision between the English and the Irish Parliaments on the Regency question was made one of the pretexts for the Union. A Bill was introduced by Mr Fitzgerald, the late Prime-Serjeant, to enact that whoever was Regent *de facto* in England should be Regent *de jure* in Ireland. Lord Castlereagh opposed it. He did not wish the difficulty to be obviated. With reference to this Bill, Lord Cornwallis, writing to the Duke of Portland, mentions several possible cases of difficulty which Lord Castlereagh will state in the House of Commons. "And as many possibilities of this kind may be stated, Lord Castlereagh will endeavour to insinuate that the only complete measure for putting an end to the difficulties which arise from the present situation of Ireland is a Parliamentary Union." Feb. 23, 1799. "Private." "Castlereagh Correspondence," ii. p. 181. Mr Lecky considers "the constitutional importance" of the Regency question to have been "greatly exaggerated." ("Leaders of Public Opinion," p. 190.) Professor Dicey is of a similar opinion. He thinks it "has been treated as possessing more importance than from a constitutional point of view belonged to it." ("Case of England against Home Rule," p. 222, note.)

[1] "Plunket's Life," i. pp. 177, 178.

without the interference of any other. That the breach of such a solemn contract, founded on the internal weakness of the country, and its inability at this time to withstand the destructive design of the Minister, must tend to destroy the harmony of both, by forming a precedent and generating a principle of mutual encroachment in times of mutual difficulties."

9. *General corruption.*

The full details of the bribery by which the Union was carried can never be ascertained. They were, of course, as far as possible, concealed at the time; and the intentional destruction of documents relating to these transactions has veiled from posterity a hideous picture of perfidy and fraud. When the promoters of the Union were charged in the British House of Lords with corruption, their accusers were taunted with the absence of evidence in support of that imputation. "With regard," says Lord Grenville, "to corruption and menace having been practised, the fair way would be to have brought proof of either, if such evidence could have been obtained."[1]

I shall confine myself to such evidence as would have satisfied the noble lord, namely, the admissions of the persons in whose hands the management of the measure lay. The extracts I cite in this connection are all taken from the "Cornwallis Correspondence," and are given in their chronological order. They will convey a faint idea of the avowed corruption by which the Union was carried, and the arts and stratagems by which it was attended. The remorseful agonies of Lord Cornwallis, and the cynical wickedness of Lord Castlereagh and the minor Castle myrmidons, are, I believe, for poignancy of contrast, unequalled in literature.

[1] April 21, 1800. Woodfall's "Parliamentary Reports," ii. p. 373.

"The political jobbing of this country," writes Lord Cornwallis, "gets the better of me. It has ever been the wish of my life to avoid all this dirty business, and I am now involved in it beyond all bearing, and am consequently more wretched than ever. I trust that I shall live to get out of this most cursed of all situations, and most repugnant to my feelings. How I long to kick those whom my public duty obliges me to court. If I did not hope to get out of this country, I would most certainly pray for immediate death."[1] A few weeks later, Lord Cornwallis writes to the same correspondent, in a tone of abject self-abasement :—" My occupation is now of the most unpleasant nature—negotiating and jobbing with the most corrupt people under heaven. I despise and hate myself every hour for engaging in such dirty work, and am supported only by the reflection that without an Union the British Empire must be dissolved. When it is impossible to gratify the unreasonable demands of our politicians, I often think of two lines of Swift, speaking of the Lord-Lieutenant and the system of corruption :—

> "' And then at Beelzebub's great hall,
> Complains his budget is too small.' "[2]

---

[1] Cornwallis to Ross, May 20, 1799. "Cornwallis Correspondence," iii. pp. 100, 101.

[2] Cornwallis to Ross, Jnue 8, 1799. "Cornwallis Correspondence," iii. p. 102. Above the door of the Chapel Royal in Dublin Castle, there is a finely executed bust of Dean Swift. It is a strange irony that the Dean's effigy should have so prominent a place in a Court which had justly aroused his "*sæva indignatio.*" The Dean came over to Ireland as domestic chaplain to the Earl of Berkeley, who was Lord Lieutenant, which probably accounts for the presence of his bust in a place which would be otherwise grimly inappropriate. The Editor of the "Cornwallis Correspondence" tells us that the lines quoted by Lord

Some Means by which the Union was carried. 147

On the 17th December 1799, Lord Castlereagh writes to the Duke of Portland : " Your Grace, I trust, will not be surprised at my requesting that you will assist us in the *same way* and to the *same extent* as you did previous to Mr Elliott's leaving London. The advantages have been important, and it is very desirable that this

---

Cornwallis are from Swift's poem, entitled, "A Libel on the Rev. Dr Delaney and His Excellency, Lord Carteret, 1729."

> " So to effect his monarch's ends,
> From Hell a Viceroy devil ascends,
> His budget with corruption crammed,
> The contributions of the damned,
> Which with unsparing hand he strows
> Through courts and senates as he goes,
> And then at Beelzebub's black hall,
> Complains his budget is too small."

The Viceregal character had not improved in Archbishop Whately's time. Here is his description of the ordinary Lord-Lieutenant given to Mr N. W. Senior, on October 9, 1852. "The Lord-Lieutenant's days and nights are wasted on intrigues and party squabbles—on the management of the press and the management of fêtes—on deciding what ruined gambler is to have this stipendiary magistracy, and what Repealer is to be conciliated by asking his wife and daughter to that concert—in short, on things nine-tenths of which cannot be so well treated as by being left alone." "Journals relating to Ireland," ii. p. 57.

The Upper Castle Yard, in which the Viceregal Apartments are situated, is known by the populace as the "Devil's half-acre." The Rev. Professor Galbraith, S.F.T.C.D., gave me the following memorandum and diagram, of which he permits me to make public use.

"The 'Devil's half-acre' is a comical name given to the Upper Castle Yard by the common people, to show their hatred and contempt for the work which has commonly been done there. I heard this from Isaac Butt, and he was much amused when I told him that I measured it by pacing, and found that the proverbial name was very nearly exact. A square of 70 yards to the side is $q.p.$ a statute acre."

	84 paces = 70 yards.	
1 military pace = 30 inches.	42 paces = 35 yards.	

request should be complied with without delay."[1] The editor of the "Cornwallis Correspondence" tells us that the assistance required was a further sum of £5000. There is a clear ring of business in the tone of this letter; all sentiment is banished to Jupiter or Saturn. A few days afterwards, the conscience-stricken Lord Cornwallis writes: "My opinions have no weight on your side of the water, and yet I am kept here to manage matters of a most disgusting nature to my feelings, merely to prevent my interfering with others in military commands."[2] "I am impatient," writes Lord Castlereagh to Mr King, "to hear from you on the subject of my letter to the Duke. We are in great distress, and I wish the transmiss was more considerable than the last. It is very important that we should not be destitute of the means on which so much depends."[3] On this letter there is a memorandum in Mr King's handwriting: "It was sent this day to Lord Castlereagh. I ventured so far as to observe to Lord Castlereagh that the fund was good security for a still further sum, though not immediately, if it could be well laid out and furnished on the spot. I trust I did not go too far."[4] When we remember that the debate in the Irish House of Commons on the Union took place on the 16th January 1800, the dates of these letters are not without their significance. Later on we find Lord Cornwallis in the slough of despond. "In the meantime I must confess that my spirits are fairly worn down, and the force which I am obliged to

---

[1] "Private and Most Secret." "Cornwallis Correspondence," iii. p. 151.
[2] December 28, 1799, Cornwallis to Ross. "Private." "Cornwallis Correspondence," iii. p. 153. Lord Cornwallis does not credit Mr Pitt and his colleagues with very elevated motives.
[3] January 2, 1800. "Private." "Cornwallis Correspondence," iii. p. 156.
[4] "Cornwallis Correspondence," iii. p. 156.

put on them in public renders me more miserable when I retire."[1] "We require *your assistance,*" writes Lord Castlereagh to Mr King, "and you *must* be prepared to enable us to fulfil the expectations which it was impossible to avoid creating at the moment of difficulty. You may be sure we have rather erred on the side of moderation." "When," enquires Mr Cooke of Mr King, "can you make the remittance promised. It is absolutely essential, for our demands increase. Pray let Lord Castlereagh know without delay what can be done by you."[3]

The death of the Archbishop of Armagh elicits the following observation of Lord Cornwallis to the Duke of Portland in urging the appointment of an Irish prelate: "I think it would have a very bad effect at this time to send a stranger to supersede the whole Bench of Bishops, and I should likewise be much embarrassed by the stop that would be put to the succession amongst the Irish Clergy at this critical period, when I am above measure pressed for ecclesiastical preferment."[4]

On the 5th April 1800 Mr Cooke is able to send cheering intelligence to Lord Castlereagh. "I have seen the Duke of Portland and Mr Pitt a second time.

[1] Cornwallis to Ross, February 4, 1800. "Cornwallis Correspondence," iii. p. 177.
[2] February 27, 1800. "Private and Secret." "Cornwallis Correspondence," iii. pp. 200, 201.
[3] March 1, 1800. "Secret." "Cornwallis Correspondence," iii. p. 202.
[4] March 11, 1800. "Private." "Cornwallis Correspondence," iii. pp. 209, 210. The Right Hon. J. T. Ball, in his recently published work, "The Reformed Church of Ireland," has severely but not unjustly characterised the scandalous system of promotion in the Establishment before the Union. As the son of an Irish clergyman, I have no hesitation in saying that Church patronage was in many cases as wickedly dispensed since the Union. The working clergy were passed over, and the high places filled by persons who reflected no credit on their position. For a glaring instance see "English in Ireland," iii. pp. 560-1.

The Duke is anxious to send you the needful. Mr Pitt was equally disposed, but fears it is impossible to the extent. He will continue to let you have £8000 to £10,000 for five years. I hope to find out to-night what sum can be sent. Mr Pitt approves of your taking advantage of the vacancies in the Civil List here. Will the law allow you to increase the Commissioners of Boards?"[1] In a later letter to Lord Castlereagh, dated London, May 6, Mr Cooke says:—"I set out for Ireland to-morrow morning. I do not come quite empty-handed."[2] On April 21, 1800, we find Lord Cornwallis as miserable as ever. "My life here," he writes, "is wretched."[3]

When the Union had been virtually carried, Lord Cornwallis writes to General Ross:—"There are too many in the Cabinet who meddle about the business of Ireland. Would to God I had done with them, Cabinet and all."[4] Again—"To myself personally and to Lord Castlereagh the winding up of the engagements is more vexatious and tormenting than any of the former part of the business."[5]

On the 10th July 1800, Mr Marsden writes to Mr Cooke:—"Lord Castlereagh wishes me remind you of the necessity of supplies. We are in great want."[6] "I hope," writes Lord Castlereagh to Mr Cooke, on 12th July 1800, "you will settle with King our further ways and means. From the best calculation I can

---

[1] "Secret" "Cornwallis Correspondence," iii. p. 226.

[2] "Secret." "Cornwallis Correspondence," iii. p. 226.

[3] Cornwallis to Rev. B. Grisdale. "Cornwallis Correspondence," iii. p. 228.

[4] June 25, 1800. "Cornwallis Correspondence," iii. p. 269.

[5] Cornwallis to Ross, July 3, 1800. "Cornwallis Correspondence, iii. p. 269.

[6] "Private." "Cornwallis Correspondence," iii. p. 276.

make, we shall *absolutely* require the remainder of what I asked for, namely, fifteen, to wind up matters, exclusive of the annual arrangement; and an immediate supply is much wanted. If it cannot be sent speedily, I hope we may discount it here." [1]

In a letter of Mr Marsden's to Mr King, dated December 9, 1800, the following passage occurs :—" I am induced to write to you from the great degree of inconvenience which I am subjected to by the delay in sending over the King's letter for putting into our hands the money saved in the Civil List in this country to be applied to Secret Service here. It has fallen to my lot to make a considerable number of the engagements which this money was to discharge, and I am pressed in some instances in the most inconvenient degree to make good my promises. There has, besides, been borrowed from a person here a considerable sum which he is extremely anxious to have repaid. The King's letter for this purpose is, I know, in the Treasury department, but as you have a superintending concern for our distresses here, I beg leave to entreat that you will have enquiry made at the Treasury about it.." "There are some other King's letters which some of our friends here are looking for rather anxiously, but money is the grand desideratum." [2]

On February 19, 1801, on the eve of his departure from Ireland, Lord Cornwallis thus writes to the Duke of Portland with reference to the "engagements which he has thought it his duty to contract on the part of His Majesty's Government, and by the directions of his Ministers repeatedly conveyed by his Grace." "Much anxiety is daily manifested by those gentlemen whose

[1] "Secret." "Cornwallis Correspondence," iii. p. 278.
[2] "Most Private." "Cornwallis Correspondence," iii. 308, 309.

expectations I have not yet been enabled to fulfil, and though I endeavour to impress on their minds an assurance that their just hopes will not be disappointed by any change in His Majesty's councils, they intimate a wish to receive that assurance from the authority of those with whom the future administration of Ireland may be connected. I am therefore to request your Grace will take the earliest opportunity of conferring with His Majesty's Ministers upon this subject, and that you will furnish me with an official authority to assure all those gentlemen who have any promise of favour in consequence of the Union, that they will be fully provided for according to the extent of the engagements made with them, and that no new pretensions will be allowed to interfere with their prior and superior claims.[1]

To this letter the editor of the "Cornwallis Correspondence" has appended the following remarks:—

"The promises alluded to in the foregoing letter were recorded in a list enclosed, which it is not considered advisable to publish *in extenso*. Of these engagements, seven were for pensions, one of which, to Mrs Young, widow of the Bishop of Clonfort, had no connection with politics. Thirteen were legal appointments, five of which were completed before Lord Cornwallis left Ireland. Four were for promotions in the Peerage. Thirty were promises of places varying from £400 to £800 per annum, or of pensions from £300 to £500. Thirty-five of the persons mentioned in this list were M.P.'s, and had voted for the Union; and three of the pensions, though granted nominally to persons not in Parliament, were actually to be received by Members. Some of these pensions and places, on account of the

[1] "Private." "Cornwallis Correspondence," iii. p. 339.

change of Government in 1806, never were conferred, but the M.P. for whose benefit one in particular was intended, came to Sir Robert Peel when Secretary in Ireland, and claimed the arrears of the pension, amounting to several thousand pounds. It is unnecessary to add that such an application was not successful. Lord Hardwicke, when he assumed the Government, recognised the engagements made by Lord Cornwallis, and, as far as he was able, fulfilled them, but he also resigned before the claimants had been satisfied, and the Duke of Bedford, who succeeded him, did not consider himself bound by the antecedent promises."[1]

On March 11th, 1801, Lord Cornwallis writes to General Ross :—"The remainder of my time here will not be pleasant, as I am dunned, without mercy, by all those who have any claims on Government for services in the late struggle."[2]

On May 6th, 1801, Mr Marsden unfolds his distresses to Mr King :—"I am again under the necessity of entreating your aid to have our money matters settled. I have already informed you how distressingly I am, more than any one, embarked in this business; and since I wrote to you nothing has been received. I wonder to see Mr A——'s secret service money so limited this year."[3]

These letters sufficiently prove that the Act of Union was carried by the aid of coarse metallic corruption.

"The Union," says the Right Honourable Richard Lalor Shiel, "was carried by corruption and by fear. The shriek of rebellion still echoed in the nation's ear. The Habeas Corpus Act had been suspended, and martial law had been proclaimed. The country was in a

---

[1] "Cornwallis Correspondence," iii. p. 349.   [2] *Ibid.*, iii. p. 349.
[3] "Private."   "Cornwallis Correspondence," iii. p. 358.

state of siege. The Minister was supplied with a purse of gold for the Senator, and a rod of iron for the people; yet that corruption, at which even Sir Robert Walpole would have been astonished, was resisted by the genius and patriotism of some of the most eminent men that this country ever produced. There was arrayed against the Minister, Grattan, Curran, Ponsonby, Foster, and almost all the distinguished men of that time, the brightest in our history."[1]

As Mr Lecky has truly observed:—"It is scarcely an exaggeration to say that the whole unbribed intellect of Ireland was opposed to the Union."[2] The means by which the Union was carried have been denounced with fierce, but not unjust indignation in the poetry of the country. The following lines, ascribed to a well-known pen, indicate the passionate resentment with which this shameful transaction is regarded by every Irishman worthy of the name:—

> "How did they pass the Union?
>   By perjury and fraud;
> By slaves who sold their land for gold,
>   As Judas sold his God.
> By all the savage acts that yet
>   Have followed England's track,
> The pitch-cap and the bayonet,
>   The gibbet and the rack.
> And thus was passed the Union
>   By Pitt and Castlereagh;
> Could Satan send, for such an end,
>   More worthy tools than they?"

---

[1] "R. v. O'Connell," p. 307.
[2] "Leaders of Public Opinion," p. 166.

CHAPTER XI.

THE COMPETENCY OF THE IRISH PARLIAMENT TO PASS THE UNION.

IN this treatise I have confined myself to the means by which the Union was carried. As, however, the competency of the Imperial Parliament to modify that measure was strongly controverted in the recent debates, it may interest the English public to know that the competency of the Irish Parliament to pass the Act of Union was still more vehemently contested. The argument of the Anti-Unionists was thus ably summarised by Mr O'Connell in 1843 : " I utterly deny the competency of the Parliament to effectuate such a measure, and I have only to appeal to the ordinary principles of delegated authority to show that a Parliament never could and never can be justified in assuming to themselves such a right as was arrogated by the Irish Parliament in passing the Act of Union. Try the question by the rules of every-day life. You employ a servant to manage your affairs, but not to supersede yourself. If you sent a servant with a horse to a fair, with directions for him to sell it there, and that instead of obeying your orders he rode away with the horse and converted the animal to his own purposes, he would be guilty of an actual felony. Now, of what is a Parliament composed if not of the servants of the public— of men sent there by the people to represent the wants and wishes of the people! The servant cannot supersede the master; he is employed for the purpose of managing the master's business; and to admit the doctrine that he would be justified in turning the master's rights and property to his own purposes, would uproot the whole social system, and when applied to matters of Government, would, of course, be equally effective in producing a revolution in the civil state. The commonsense of every man tells him that the delegate can never supersede much less destroy the principal.

" Upon this subject I have the opinions of the highest authorities upon my side. Lord Grey (then Mr Charles Grey), said in the British House of Commons: ' Though you should be able to carry the measure, the people of Ireland would wait for an opportunity of RECOVERING THEIR RIGHTS, which they will say were taken from them by force.' This sentence does not, I admit, actually decide the point; it, however, strongly implies that the RIGHTS of the people of Ireland could not thus be taken away from them. But I can appeal to authority more potent by far than even Lord Grey, to whose words I do not in the present instance attach paramount importance, for I can quote in favour of my position from Locke's celebrated treatise upon Government, which was a class-book in (Trinity) College at the time that the honourable and learned gentleman (Mr Butt[1]) was in the University. The

---

[1] Mr Butt, who lived to be the leader of the Irish Parliamentary party, and the enthusiastic advocate of Home Rule, opposed, in the Dublin Corporation in 1843, Mr O'Connell's motion in favour of Repeal. Mr O'Connell's great penetration enabled him to predict with confidence that Mr Butt would yet be an apostle of Irish Nationality. " I watched to see if Alderman Butt would say anything to commit him against being the friend of Repeal hereafter, and I have the satisfaction to tell you that he is as free

testimony of such a man as Locke upon such a subject as the present must be of inconceivable importance; for Locke was a man cherished by the Irish Orange party—he was the apostle of the Revolution of 1688, and was the writer who was the most successful in rallying public opinion in favour of that Revolution. To his writings is eminently due the consolidation of that most important political alteration, and to the work in particular which I now quote, is that effect principally traceable. This work was also a text-book in our University (of Dublin) until, I am told, a late period, when, it is said, his book was dismissed from the College course, on account, perhaps, of the piece of honesty of which he had been guilty in giving expression to the following judgment. 'The legislature (he says) cannot transfer the power of making laws into other hands, for it being but a delegated power from the people, they who have it cannot pass it over to others. The people alone can appoint the form of the commonwealth, which is by constituting the legislature and appointing in whose hands that shall be; and when the people will have said we submit, and will be governed by laws made by such men, and in such terms, nobody else can say other men shall make laws for them. The power of the legislature being derived from the people by a positive voluntary grant and institution can be no other than what the positive grant conveyed, which being only to make laws and not to make legislatures, the legislature can have no power to

to support Repeal if he should think fit to do so as I am. A man of his genius must have some yearning for his native land, and although the word Ireland may not sound as musically in his ear as in mine, depend upon it that Alderman Butt is in his inmost soul an Irishman, and that we will have him struggling with us for Ireland yet."

transfer their authority of making laws, or to place it in other hands.' But if this authority be not of sufficiently modern date, what will you say to the words of William Saurin, the chief and champion of the Anti-Catholic party in Ireland, a man of first-rate abilities, who actually governed by his councils that party, and through its means Ireland, for more than twenty years. He also was another great favourite of my opponents, who declared, 'You may make the Union binding as a law, but you cannot make it obligatory on conscience. It will be obeyed so long as England is strong, but resistance to it will be in the abstract a duty, and the exhibition of that resistance will be a mere question of prudence.'[1] Listen now to another great authority. Lord Chancellor Plunket, in addressing the House of Commons, said, 'Sir, I, in the most express terms, deny the competency of Parliament to do this act. I warn you; do not lay your hands on the constitution. I tell you that if, circumstanced as you are, you pass this Act, it will be a mere nullity, and no man in Ireland will be bound to obey it. I make the assertion deliberately. I repeat it. I call on every man who hears me to take down my words. You have not been elected for this purpose. You are appointed to make laws, not legislatures—you are appointed to exercise the functions of legislators and not to transfer them—you are appointed to act under the constitution and not to alter it; and if you do so, your act is a dissolution of Government — you resolve society into its original elements, and no man in the land is bound to obey you. Sir, I state doctrines which are not merely founded on the immutable laws of truth and reason. I state not

[1] Mr Saurin was Attorney-General for Ireland for upwards of twenty years. He was offered, but declined, the post of Chief-Justice of Ireland

merely the opinions of the ablest and wisest men who have written on the science of Government, but I state the practice of our constitution, as settled at the era of the Revolution; and I state the doctrine under which the House of Hanover derives its title to the throne. Has the King a right to transfer his crown? Is he competent to annex it to the crown of Spain, or any other country? No, but he may abdicate it; and every man who knows the constitution knows the consequence—the right reverts to the next in succession. If they all abdicate, it reverts to the people. The man who questions this doctrine, in the same breath must arraign the sovereign on the throne as an usurper. Are you competent to transfer your legislative rights to the French Council of Five Hundred? Are you competent to transfer them to the British Parliament? I answer, No. If you transfer you abdicate, and the great original trust reverts to the people, from whom it issued. Yourselves you may extinguish, but Parliament you cannot extinguish. It is enthroned in the hearts of the people—it is enshrined in the sanctuary of the constitution—it is as immortal as the island which it protects. As well might the frantic suicide hope that the act which destroys his miserable body would extinguish his eternal soul! Again I therefore warn you. Do not dare to lay your hands on the constitution—it is above your power.'"[1]

[1] "Discussion in Dublin Corporation on the Repeal of the Union," pp. 34-36.

APPENDIX A. (p. 73).

LORD CASTLEREAGH AND MARTIAL LAW.

ON the breaking out of the Rebellion in 1798, Lord Pery suggested the advisability of an Act of Parliament authorising the military authorities to try by court martial persons engaged in the insurrection. Referring to "Lord Pery's idea," Lord Castlereagh says: "It was before resisted upon the principle that there was less violence done to the Constitution in giving indemnity to those who have acted illegally for the preservation of the State than in enacting laws so adverse to the usual spirit of our legislature. This consideration prevailed, and were the struggle but of short duration, perhaps the inconvenience would be trifling; but if it is to be procrastinated, which there is too much reason to apprehend may be the case in this kingdom where religious resentment, as well as principles of resistance, are so deeply and extensively implanted, it is a question whether military authority in some degree is not requisite to keep society together, and if so, the responsibility of doing an act which, in the eye of the law, is in strictness murder is too weighty to be encountered in the prospect of future indemnity.

"I trust, however, that the internal situation of the country may improve now the prospect of foreign assistance is in a great measure at an end, and that we may be saved from an alternative so unpleasant as that of yielding to this tormenting evil rather than risk the adoption of a strong remedy, or of being driven to extend the powers of a military code to civil crimes, if crimes can be called civil which are invariably committed in arms."—"Castlereagh Correspondence," p. 447.

Appendix.

Lord Castlereagh wrote this letter, which he expected might "meet the Duke of Portland's eye," within a month after Lord Cornwallis' censure of the members of Whollaghan Court Martial (pp. 63, 64).

It is, I think, no injustice to his lordship's memory to say that with full experience of the method in which martial law was administered in Ireland he desired to fence that system with statutory protection, and to place those murderous tribunals—the Courts Martial—in a position of greater freedom and less responsibility.

Turnbull & Spears, Printers, Edinburgh.

www.ingramcontent.com/pod-product-compliance
Lightning Source LLC
Chambersburg PA
CBHW030244170426
43202CB00009B/619